Personal Interview Skills

Personal Interview Skills

Krishan Kumar

The Readers Paradise
New Delhi - 110002

Personal Interview Skills
Krishan Kumar

First Edition

ISBN - 978-81-938231-0-1

Published by
The Readers Paradise
103, 4787/23, Ansari Road,
Darya Ganj, New Delhi - 110002
09654444181
thereadersparadisesales@gmail.com
www.thereadersparadise.com

Page No. - 232 | Paper - 80gsm
Size - 5.5x8.5

Typesetting & Cover Design by
Sanya Computers

Preface

Welcome to Interview Skills: your new definitive guide on how to pass a job interview. This guide has been designed to help you prepare for and pass any type of job interview. The author of this guide, Richard McMinn, has been successful at over 95% of interviews he has attended. You will find his guidance both highly informative and an invaluable tool in your pursuit to passing your job interview. Interviews can be a very nerve-wracking experience. The way to overcome those nerves is to embark on a period of intensive preparation in the build up to your interview. The majority of employers will assess you predominantly against the job description or the person specification for the job that you are applying for. Whilst reading this guide we advise that you have a copy of these important documents at your side. If you would like any further assistance with your preparation for any kind of job interview, assessment centre or selection process, then we offer a wide range or products and training courses at the website: www.how2become.co.uk finally, you won't achieve much in life without hard work, determination and perseverance. Work hard, stay focused and be what you want!

For the vast majority of people, interviews are a nerve-wracking experience. At the very least, they are something that you could probably do without, right? This book is aimed at changing your entire mindset towards interviews and, more importantly, making you believe that success is in your own hands. I've enjoyed a fantastic career during my life so far. I've been an Aircraft Engineer in the Royal Navy, an Officer in the Fire Service and now an entrepreneur and published author. I left school with very few qualifications but I was determined not to let this lack of educational achievement get in the way of being successful. During my time in the Fire Service I passed many promotional interviews. I was successful at over 95% of interviews that I attended. My success wasn't down to luck, or some miracle 'interview success gene', but rather adopting the correct approach to both my interview preparation and also the interview itself. During this guide I will teach you how to implement my success formula into your own life. I suggest that you use it every time you go to interview. The majority of people believe that you have to answer every interview question correctly in order to get the job. This couldn't be further from the truth. Yes it is important to demonstrate during an interview that you have both the subject knowledge of the role you are applying for, and also knowledge about the organisation you are applying to join, but it is just as important to work on your interview technique and your 'likeability' factor. When I prepare for any interview I will always split my preparation up into three different areas. These are:

- Interview technique
- Research
- Responding to the interview questions

If I work on all of these three elements in equal measures, then I will have the confidence and knowledge to pass the interview. When I walk through that door into the interview room, I only have one thing on my mind – impressing the panel sufficiently that they will have to give me the job! During this guide I will teach you how to comprehensively cover all three of these areas. So, you will probably be able to tell that my mindset, both prior and during the interview, is one of confidence and self-belief. These two factors are very important in helping you to pass the interview. By the time you've finished reading this guide you will have both of them, and in copious amounts too. I strongly believe that passing interviews is like riding a bike – once you know how it never leaves you. Take the time to study the contents of this guide carefully, and then go and pass your interview with flying colours!

Contents

Chapter 1

Recruitment-Core functions of human resource management; 7–27

Chapter 2

Interview of candidate – one-on-one conversation; 28–36

Chapter 3

Developing your Personal Themes; 37–48

Chapter 4

Interacting effectively with the Interviewer; 49–61

Chapter 5

Navigating the dynamics of interview conversations; 62–68

Chapter 6

The Essential Interview questions 69–128

Chapter 7

50 Smashes 129–154

Chapter 8

Win the Deal 155–158

Chapter 9

The Final Negotiation 159–164

Chapter 10

Relational Interview skills 165–230

CHAPTER 1

Recruitment-Core function of human resource management

Recruitment is a core function of human resource management. It is the first step of appointment. Recruitment refers to the overall process of attracting, selecting and appointing suitable candidates for jobs within an organization. Recruitment can also refer to processes involved in choosing individuals for unpaid positions, such as voluntary roles or unpaid trainee roles. Managers, human resource generalists and recruitment specialists may be tasked with carrying out recruitment, but in some cases public-sector employment agencies, commercial recruitment agencies, or specialist search consultancies are used to undertake parts of the process. Internet-based technologies to support all aspects of recruitment have become widespread.

Recruitment is the process of finding and hiring the best-qualified candidate for a job opening, in a timely and cost effective manner. The recruitment process includes analyzing the requirements of a job, attracting employees to that job, screening and selecting applicants, hiring, and integrating the new employee to the organization.

Recruitment is a core function of human resource management. Recruitment refers to the overall process of attracting, selecting and appointing suitable candidates for jobs within an organization. Recruitment can also refer to processes involved in choosing individuals for unpaid positions, such as voluntary roles or unpaid trainee roles. Managers, human resource generalists and recruitment specialists may be tasked with carrying out recruitment, but in some cases public-sector employment agencies, commercial recruitment agencies, or specialist search consultancies are used to undertake parts of the process. Internet-based technologies to support all aspects of recruitment have become widespread.

Job analysis

In situations where multiple new jobs are created and recruited for the first time or vacancies are there or the nature in such documents as job descriptions and job specifications Often, a company already has job descriptions for existing positions. Where already drawn up, these documents may require review and updating to reflect current requirements. Prior to the recruitment stage, a person specification should be finalized.

Sourcing

Sourcing is the use of one or more strategies to attract or identify candidates to fill job vacancies. It may involve internal and/or external recruitment advertising, using appropriate media, such as job portals, local or national newspapers, social media, business media, specialist recruitment media, professional publications, window advertisements, job centers, or in a variety of ways via the internet.

Alternatively, employers may use recruitment consultancies or agencies to find otherwise scarce candidates—who, in many cases, may be content in their current positions and are not actively looking to move. This initial research for candidates—also called name generation—produces contact information for potential candidates, whom the recruiter can then discreetly contact and screen.

Screening and selection

Various psychological tests can assess a variety of KSAOs, including literacy. Assessments are also available to measure physical ability. Recruiters and agencies may use applicant tracking systems to filter candidates, along with software tools for psychometric testing and performance-based assessment. In many countries, employers are legally mandated to ensure their screening and selection processes meet equal opportunity and ethical standards.

Employers are likely to recognize the value of candidates who encompass soft skills such as interpersonal or team leadership. Many companies, including multinational organizations and those that recruit from a range of nationalities, are also often concerned about whether candidate fits the prevailing company culture.

Disabled candidates

The word disability carries few positive connotations for most employers. Research has shown that employer biases tend to improve through first-hand experience and exposure with proper supports for the employee and the employer making the hiring decisions. As for most companies, money and job stability are two of the contributing factors to the productivity of a disabled employee, which in return equates to the growth and success of a business. Hiring disabled workers produce more advantages than disadvantages. There is no difference in the daily production of a disabled worker. Given their situation, they are more likely to adapt to their environmental surroundings and acquaint themselves with equipment, enabling them to solve problems and overcome adversity as with other employees. The U.S. IRS grants companies Disabled Access Credit when they meet eligibility criteria.

Diversity

Many major corporations recognize the need for diversity in hiring to compete successfully in a global economy. Other organizations, for example universities and colleges, have been slow to embrace diversity as an essential value for their success.

Recruitment Process Outsourcing (RPO)

Recruitment Process Outsourcing, or commonly known as "RPO" is a form of business process outsourcing (BPO) where a company engages a third party provider to manage all or part of its recruitment process.

Approaches

Internal recruitment (not to be confused with internal recruiters!) refers to the process of a candidate being selected from the existing workforce to take up a new job in the same organization, perhaps as a promotion, or to provide career development opportunity, or to meet a specific or urgent organizational need. Advantages include the organization's familiarity with the employee and their competencies insofar as they are revealed in their current job, and their willingness to trust said employee. It can be quicker and have a lower cost to hire someone internally.

An employee referral program is a system where existing employees recommend prospective candidates for the job offered, and in some organizations if the suggested candidate is hired, the employee receives a cash bonus.

Niche firms tend to focus on building ongoing relationships with their candidates, as the same candidates may be placed many times throughout their careers. Online resources have developed to help find niche recruiters. Niche firms also develop knowledge on specific employment trends within their industry of focus (e.g., the energy industry) and are able to identify demographic shifts such as aging and its impact on the industry.

Social recruiting is the use of social media for recruiting including sites like Facebook and twitter or career-oriented social networking sites such as LinkedIn and XING. It is a rapidly growing sourcing technique, especially with middle-aged people. On Google+, the fastest-growing age group is 45–54. On Twitter, the expanding generation is people from ages 55–64.

Mobile recruiting is a recruitment strategy that uses mobile technology to attract, engage and convert candidates. Mobile recruiting is often cited as a growing opportunity for recruiters to connect with candidates more efficiently with "over 89% of job seekers saying their mobile device will be an important tool and resource for their job search."

Some recruiters work by accepting payments from job seekers, and in return helps them to find a job. This is illegal in some countries, such as in the United Kingdom, in which recruiters must not charge candidates for their services. Such recruiters often refer to themselves as "personal marketers" and "job application services" rather than as recruiters.

Using Multiple-criteria decision analysis tools such as Analytic Hierarchy Process (AHP) and combining it with conventional recruitment methods provides an added advantage by helping the recruiters to make decisions when there are several diverse criteria to be considered or when the applicants lack past experience; for instance recruitment of fresh university graduates.

Multi Tier Recruitment Model

In some companies where the recruitment volume is high, it is common to see a multi tier recruitment model where the different sub-functions are being group together to achieve efficiency.

An example of a 3 tier recruitment model:

Tier 1 — Contact/ Help desk - This tier acts as the first point of contact where recruitment requests are being raised. If the requests are simple to fulfil or are queries in nature, resolution may take place at this tier

Tier 2 — Administration - This tier manages mainly the administration processes

Tier 3 — Process - This tier manages the process and how the requests get fulfilled

Sourcing

Sourcing is the use of one or more strategies to attract or identify candidates to fill job vacancies. It may involve internal and/or external recruitment advertising, using appropriate media, such as job portals, local or national newspapers, social media, business media, specialist recruitment media, professional publications, window advertisements, job centres, or in a variety of ways via the internet.

Alternatively, employers may use recruitment consultancies or agencies to find otherwise scarce candidates—who, in many cases, may be content in their current positions and are not actively looking to move. This initial research for candidates—also called name generation—produces contact information for potential candidates, whom the recruiter can then discreetly contact and screen.

Screening and selection

Various psychological tests can assess a variety of KSAOs, including literacy. Assessments are also available to measure physical ability. Recruiters and agencies may use applicant tracking systems to filter candidates, along with software tools for psychometric testing and performance-based assessment. In many countries, employers are legally mandated to ensure their screening and selection processes meet equal opportunity and ethical standards.

Employers are likely to recognize the value of candidates who encompass soft skills such as interpersonal or team leadership. Many companies, including multinational organizations and those recruit from a range of nationalities, are also often concerned about whether candidate fits the prevailing company culture.

Personnel Selection

Personnel selection is the methodical process used to hire individuals. Although the term can apply to all aspects of the process the most common meaning focuses on the selection of workers. In this respect, selected prospects are separated from rejected applicants with the intention of choosing the person who will be the most successful and make the most valuable contributions to the organization. Its effect on the group is discerned when the selected accomplish their desired impact to the group, through achievement or tenure. The procedure of selection takes after strategy to gather data around a person so as to figure out whether that individual ought to be utilized. The strategies used must be in compliance with the various laws in respect to work force selection.

The professional standards of industrial-organizational psychologists require that any selection system be based on a job analysis to ensure that the selection criteria are job-related. The requirements for a selection system are characteristics known as KSAOs – knowledge, skills, ability, and other characteristics. US law also recognizes bona fide occupational qualifications, which are requirements for a job which would be considered discriminatory if not necessary – such as only employing men as wardens of maximum-security male prisons, enforcing a mandatory retirement age for airline pilots, or a religious college only employing professors of its religion to teach its theology.

Personnel selection systems employ evidence-based practices to determine the most qualified candidates and involve both the newly hired and those individuals who can be promoted from within the organization.

In this respect, selection of personnel has "validity" if an unmistakable relationship can be shown between the system itself and the employment for which the people are ultimately being chosen for. In this way, a vital piece of selection is Job Analysis. An analysis is typically conducted before, and regularly apart of, the improvement in determination systems. Then again, a selection method may be deemed valid after it has already been executed by directing follow up job analysis and demonstrating the relationship between the selection process and the respective job.

The procedure of personnel selection includes gathering data about the potential candidates with the end goal of deciding suitability and sustainability for the employment in that particular job. This data is gathered utilizing one or more determination devices or strategies classified as such:

- Interviews
- Personality Tests
- Biographical Data
- Cognitive Ability Tests
- Physical Ability Tests

Work Samples

Development and implementation of such screening methods is sometimes done by human resources departments; larger organizations hire consultants or firms that specialize in developing personnel selection systems. I-O psychologists must evaluate evidence regarding the extent to which selection tools predict job performance, evidence that bears on the validity of selection tools. These procedures are usually validated, using one or more of the following types of validity: content validity, construct validity, and/or criterion-related validity.

History and development

Chinese civil servant exams, established in AD 605, may be the first documented "modern" selection tests, and have influenced subsequent examination systems. As a scientific and scholarly field, personnel selection owes much too psychometric theory and the art of integrating selection systems falls to human resource professionals.

In the United States of America, members of the Society for Industrial and Organizational Psychology (SIOP) conduct much of the research on selection. Primary research topics include: the practicality, reliability, validity, and utility of various forms of selection measures methods for demonstrating return on investment for selection systems assessing fairness and making selection systems as fair as possible legal issues—such as disparate treatment and disparate impact—and overall compliance with laws the generalizability of validity across different work contexts alternative methods of demonstrating validity, such as synthetic validity the predictive validity of non-traditional measures, such as personality

Types of selection measures

Industrial and organizational (I–O) psychologists and hiring managers use a variety of measures to select applicants who are the best fit for a position. The main goal of these tests is to predict job performance, and each test has its own relative strengths and weaknesses in this regard. When making a hiring decision, it is critical to understand the applicant's personality style, values, motivations, and attitudes. Technical competency can be acquired by new employees, but personality is engrained in individuals.

Interviews

Interviews are one of the most common ways that individuals are selected. The best interviews follow a structured framework in which each applicant is asked the same questions and is scored with a standardized rating scale. In this way, structured interviews provide more reliable results than unstructured interviews.

Types of interviews

Unstructured Interview involves a procedure where different questions may be asked of different applicants.

Situational Interview: Candidates are interviewed about what actions they would take in various job-related situations. The job-related situations are usually identified using the critical incidents job analysis technique. The interviews are then scored using a scoring guide constructed by job experts.

Behaviour Description Interviews: Candidates are asked what actions they have taken in prior job situations that are similar to situations they may encounter on the job. The interviews are then scored using a scoring guide constructed by job experts.

Comprehensive Structured Interviews: Candidates are asked questions pertaining to how they would handle job-related situations, job knowledge, worker requirements, and how the candidate would perform various job simulations. Interviews tapping job knowledge offer a way to assess a candidate's current level of knowledge related to relevant implicit dimensions of job performance.

Structured Behavioural Interview: This technique involves asking all interviewees standardized questions about how they handled past situations that were similar to situations they may encounter on the job. The interviewer may also ask discretionary probing questions for details of the situations, the interviewee's behaviour in the situation and the outcome. The interviewee's responses are then scored with behaviourally anchored rating scales.

Oral Interview Boards: This technique entails the job candidate giving oral responses to job-related questions asked by a panel of interviewers. Each member of the panel then rates each interviewee on such dimensions as work history, motivation, creative thinking, and presentation. The scoring procedure for oral interview boards has typically been subjective; thus, it would be subject to personal biases of those individuals sitting on the board. This technique may not be feasible for jobs in which there are a large number of applicants that must be interviewed.

Personality testing

Another tool used for selection is personality testing. Personality tests can provide an accurate analysis of an applicant's attitudes and interpersonal skills. These tests can reveal a variety of things about an applicant, such as how well the applicant gets along with others, self-discipline, attention to detail, organization, flexibility, and disposition.

Types of personality tests

Personal Attribute Inventory: An interpersonal assessment instrument which consists of 50 positive and 50 negative adjectives from Gough's Adjective Check List. The subject is to select 30 which are most descriptive of the target group or person in question. This instrument was specifically designed to tap affective reactions and may be used in either assessing attitudes toward others or as a self-concept scale.

Personality Adjective Checklist: A comprehensive, objective measure of eight personality styles. These eight personality styles are: extroversive, inhibited, cooperative, sociable, confident, forceful, respectful, and sensitive. This instrument is designed for use with non psychiatric patients and normal adults who read minimally at the eighth grade level. Test reports are computer-generated and are intended for use by qualified professionals only. Interpretive statements are based on empirical data and theoretical inference. They are considered probabilistic in nature and cannot be considered definitive.

Cross-Cultural Adaptability Inventory: Self-scoring six-point rating scale is a training instrument designed to provide feedback to individuals about their potential for cross-cultural effectiveness. It is most effective when used as part of a training program. It can also be used as a team-building tool for culturally diverse work groups and as a counselling tool for people in the process of cross-cultural adjustment. The inventory contains 50 items, distributed among 4 subscales: emotional resilience, flexibility/openness, perceptual acuity, personal autonomy.

California Psychological Inventory: Multipurpose questionnaire designed to assess normal personality characteristics important in everyday life that individuals make use of to understand, classify, and predict their own behaviours and that of others. In this revision, two new scales, empathy and independence, have been added; semantic changes were made in 29 items; and 18 items were eliminated. The inventory is applicable for use in a variety of settings, including business and industry, schools and colleges, clinics and counselling agencies, and for cross cultural and other research. It may be used to advise employees/applicants about their vocational plans.

Biographical data selection

Background Information/Application: - Blanks Paper-and-pencil questionnaires, interviews, and communications with past employers in order to assess an individual's behavioural reliability, integrity, and personal adjustment. In order to implement this technique a validation study would have to be conducted.

Empirically-keyed Bio data: Applicants are presented with a list of questions pertaining to such things as one's economic stability, work ethic orientation, and educational achievement. Applicants' scores are determined by weighting each item according to the item's empirically derived relationship to the criterion of interest. This technique requires a validation study to be carried out in order to obtain the empirically derived weights for the bio data.

Rationally-keyed Bio data: Applicants are presented with a list of questions pertaining to such things as one's economic stability, work ethic orientation and educational achievement. Applicants' scores are determined by weighting each item according to the item's rationally derived relationship to the criterion of interest. Research indicates the predictive validity of this technique may be lower than other available techniques with no evidence for reduced adverse impact against minorities.

Ability tests

Psychomotor-ability tests are used to measure fine motor skills and hand-eye coordination. These skills are important in jobs, like carpentry, that require a lot of hand-eye coordination. Unlike psychomotor ability tests, physical ability tests measure gross motor skills, such as lifting and running. These skills are important in jobs such as construction, where strength is needed.

Cognitive ability tests

Employee Aptitude Survey: A battery of employment tests designed to meet the practical requirements of a personnel office. It consists of 10 cognitive, perceptual, and psychomotor ability tests. Nine of the 10 tests have 5-minute time limits. The remaining test requires two to ten minutes of testing time. Is a tool for personnel selection and a useful diagnostic tool for vocational guidance and career counselling. For situations in which it is desirable to retest an individual on an alternate form, special retest norms are provided for interpreting retest scores.

Test 1 – Verbal Comprehension: Each item consists of one word in capital letters followed by four words in small letters. The respondent is to choose the word in small letters that means about the same as the word in capital letters. Scoring is the number rights minus 1/3 the number wrong.

Test 2 – Numerical Ability: A battery of three tests: integers, decimal fractions and common fractions, each is timed separately. It has designed to measure skill in the four basic operations of addition, subtraction, multiplication, and division.

Test 3 – Visual Pursuit: Designed to measure the ability to make rapid scanning movements of the eyes without being distracted by other irrelevant visual stimulation. It involves the visual tracing of lines through an entangled network.

Test 4 – Visual Speed and Accuracy: The test consists of two columns of numbers; the respondent decides whether the number in the first column in exactly the same as the number in the second.

Test 5 – Space Visualization: Designed to measure the ability to visualize forms in space and to manipulate these forms or objects mentally. The test taker is shown a group of numbered, piled blocks and must determine, for a specifically numbered block, how many other blocks touch it.

Test 6 – Numerical Reasoning: Designed to measure the ability to analyze logical relationships and to see the underlying principles of such relationships. This is also known as the process of inductive reasoning—making generalizations from specific instances. The test taker is given a series of numbers and determines what the next number will be. Scoring is the number rights minus 1/4 the number wrong.

Test 7 – Verbal Reasoning Revised: Designed to measure the ability to analyze verbally stated facts and to make valid judgments on the basis of the logical implications of such facts; and thus, the ability to analyze available information in order to make practical decisions. Scoring is the number of right answers minus 1/2 the wrong answers.

Test 8 – Word Fluency: Designed to measure the ability to express oneself rapidly, easily and with flexibility. Word fluency involves the speed and freedom of word usage as opposed to understanding verbal meanings. People who measure high in this ability are particularly good at expressing themselves and in finding the right word at the right time. The test taker is given a letter of the alphabet and asked to write as many words as possible that begin with that letter.

Test 9 – Manual Speed and Accuracy: Designed to measure the ability to make rapid and precise movements with the hands and fingers. Also measures, according to the authors, the temperamental willingness to perform highly repetitive, routine, and monotonous work. The test taker is to put a pencil dot in as many circles as he or she can in five minutes, without letting the dots touch the sides of the small circles.

Test 10 – Symbolic Reasoning: Designed to measure the ability to think and reason abstractly, using symbols rather than words or numbers; to manipulate abstract symbols mentally; and to make judgments and decisions which are logical and valid. Each problem contains a statement and a conclusion and uses certain symbols such as the equal sign and mathematical symbols for greater than and smaller than, etc. The test taker determines whether the conclusion is definitely true, definitely false, or impossible to determine on the basis of the statement. Scoring is the number of right answers minus 1/2 the wrong answers.

Progressive Matrices, Advanced Sets I and II. A nonverbal test designed for use as an aid in assessing mental ability. It requires the examinee to solve problems presented in abstract figures and designs. Scores are said to correlate well with comprehensive intelligence tests. Set II provides a means of assessing all the analytical and integral operations involved in the higher thought processes and differentiates between people of superior intellectual ability.

Kaufman Brief Intelligence Test. Brief individually administered measure of verbal and nonverbal intelligence for people aged 4–90. Developed specifically for screening purposes and for those situations where it would be difficult to do a more in-depth assessment. Norms are provided for all ages. It is composed of two subtests, vocabulary and matrices. Vocabulary measures verbal, school-related skills by assessing word knowledge and verbal concept formation. Matrices measures nonverbal skills and ability to solve new problems. Items in matrices subtest involve pictures and designs.

Short-term Memory Tests A form of cognitive ability test that are exemplified by short-term memory tasks such as forward digit span and serial rote learning, which do not require mental manipulation of inputs in order to provide an output. Short-term memory tests lack face validity in predicting job performance.

Information Processing Tests Selection tests that have the same information processing requirements that occur on the job. In other words, the tests are tailored for each particular job. There is some evidence that adverse impact is reduced.

Physical ability tests

Fitness for the job – Rejection of an applicant for failing a physical abilities test must be based on a determination of the individual's fitness for the job not on a general determination on the disabilities of the applicant.

Liability – Although a physician may administer the physical abilities test, it is the employer who decides to hire or not, therefore the liability for violations of Title VII or ADA will rest with the employer.

Work sample

Another selection technique is to have the applicant complete a hiring assignment. The applicant is asked to complete a task that simulates the actual job. The goal is to assess how well the applicant can learn and perform the tasks. This is common practice for engineering jobs.

Types of work sample tests

Work-Sample Tests of Trainability: These are tests through a period of instruction when the applicant is expected to learn tasks involved in a work sample. The work-sample tests of trainability are suitable for untrained applicants with no previous job experience. The predictive validity of this technique is low relative to other techniques and there is evidence the validity of the instrument may attenuate over time.

Simulation of an Event: These tests present the candidate with a picture of an incident along with quotations from those involved. The candidates then respond to a series of questions in which they write down the decisions they would make. The test is scored by subject matter experts.

Low Fidelity Simulations: These tests present applicants with descriptions of work situations and five alternative responses for each situation. Applicants choose the responses they would most likely and least likely make in each situation.

Work-samples Applicants perform observable, job-related behaviours as predictors of criterion performance. It is not feasible to adapt certain work behaviours for testing. Work samples often are not conducive to group administration and, therefore, were dropped from consideration because of concerns regarding test security.

Validating Work Sample Tests

Content Validity: The most direct relationship between the test and job would be shown through content validation. The tasks and duties performed on the test would be compared to the tasks and duties performed on the job. The test should encompass significant (in quantity or in importance) tasks/duties of the job.

Criterion Validity: To measure this validity, you must first determine what criteria will be used. Two common forms of criteria are:

Supervisory ratings of the incumbent's job performance. The disadvantage of using supervisory ratings as criteria is that they typically lack sufficient reliability to be used for statistical analysis. The reliability of these measures is attenuated by rater errors such as 'halo' or 'leniency'. These ratings alto tend to lack the variability necessary to show a correlation between predictor and criterion.

Production measures such as quantity or quality of work. Production measures are not available for some jobs. The predictor measures used with work sample tests include:

- Number of work samples completed (using a time limit)
- Time to complete work samples
- Number and type of errors

Validity and reliability

I–O psychologists must evaluate the validity of these measures in order to determine the extent to which selection tools can predict job performance. Measures have different types of validity that capture different qualities. There are three major types of validity: content validity, construct validity, and criterion validity.

Content validity

Content validity refers to how comprehensively the measure assesses the underlying construct that it claims to assess. As an example, let's look at a job interview for a position as a banker. This measure would have low content validity if it assessed whether the candidate was comfortable talking to many different people but not whether they were comfortable with math, because the candidate would not have been thoroughly evaluated on every facet of being a banker. The measure didn't cover the full breadth of what the job requires.

Construct validity

Construct validity refers to whether the measure accurately assesses the underlying construct that it claims to assess. This can be evaluated by examining correlations with other measures that purport to assess the same construct. When we ask if a measure has good construct validity, we're asking, "does this test the thing we are interested in testing?" An example of a measure with debatable construct validity is IQ testing. It is intended to measure intelligence, but there is disagreement about whether it measures intelligence, as it claims, or merely one type of skill.

Criterion validity

Criterion validity examines how well the construct correlates with one's behaviour in the real world across multiple situations and manifestations. For instance, does the measure adequately capture the construct as it presents in real life.

Reliability

The reliability of a measure refers to whether the measure gets repeatable results. Will the recruitment and selection processes that a company uses work every time they need to hire someone, or just once? If their processes get good results every time, those measures can be said to be reliable.

Validity of interviews

The validity of interviews describes how useful interviews are in predicting job performance. In one of the most comprehensive meta-analytic summary to date was by Weisner and Cronshaw. The authors investigated interview validity as a function of interview format and degree of structure. Results of this study showed that structured interviews yielded much higher mean corrected validities than unstructured interviews (0.63 vs. 0.20), and structured board interviews using consensus ratings had the highest corrected validity (0.64).

In McDaniel, Wetzel, Schmidt & Maurer's Comprehensive Review and Meta- analysis of the Validity of Interviews paper, the authors go a step further and include an examination of the validity of three different types of interview content. Their goal was to explore the possibility that validity is a function of the type of content collected.

They define the three kinds of content as follows – situational content was described as interview questions that get information on how the interviewee would behave in specific situations presented by the interviewer. For example, a question that asks whether the interviewee would choose to report a co-worker for behaving in an unethical way or just let them goes. Job related questions, on the other hand, assess the interviewee's past behaviour and job-related information. While psychological interviews include questions intended to assess the interviewee's personality traits such as their work ethic, dependability, honesty etc.

The authors conducted a meta-analysis of all previous studies on the validity of interviews across the three types of content mentioned above. Their results show that for job-performance criteria, situational interviews yield higher mean validity (0.50) than do job-related interviews (0.39) which yield a higher mean validity than do psychology interviews (0.29). This means that when the interview is used to predict job performance, it is best to conduct situational interviews rather than job-related or psychological interviews. On the other hand, when interviews are used to predict an applicant's training performance, the mean validity of job-related interviews (0.36) is somewhat lower than the mean validity of psychological interviews (0.40).

Going beyond the content of the interview, the authors' analysis of interview validity was extended to include an assessment of how the interview was conducted. Here, two questions emerged – Are structured interviews more valid than unstructured interviews and are board interviews more valid than individual interviews.

Their answer to the first question – Are structured interviews more valid unstructured interviews was that structured interviews, regardless of content, is more valid (0.44) than unstructured interviews (0.33) in predicting job performance criteria. However, when training performance is the criteria, the validity of structured and unstructured interviews is similar (0.34 and 0.36).

As for the validity of board interviews versus individual interviews, the researchers conducted another meta-analysis comparing the validity of board interviews and individual interviews for job performance criteria. The results show that individual interviews are more valid than board interviews (0.43 vs. 0.32). This is true regardless of whether the individual interview is structured or unstructured.

When exploring the variance in interview validity between job performance, training performance, and tenure criteria, the researchers found that the interviews are similar in predictive accuracy for job-performance and training performance (0.37 vs 0.36). But less predictive is for tenure (0.20).

Validity of cognitive ability and personality tests

Based on meta-analysis results, cognitive ability tests appear to be among the most valid of all psychological tests and are valid for most occupations. However, these tests tend to do better at predicting training criteria than long term job performance. Cognitive ability tests in general provide the benefit of being generalizable. Hence they can be used across organizations and jobs and have been shown to produce large economic gains for companies that use them.

But despite the high validity of cognitive testing, it is less frequently used as selection tools. One main reason is that cognitive ability testing has been demonstrated to produce adverse impact. In general, groups including Hispanics and African-Americans score lower than the general population while other groups including Asian – Americans score higher. The legal issues with cognitive ability testing were amplified by the Supreme Court's ruling in the famous 1971 Griggs v. Duke Power case. In this case, the Supreme Court ruled that when a selection test produces adverse impact against protected group members the company must be able to defend it by showing that use of the test is a "business necessity" for the operation of the business. The courts have held narrow interpretations of business necessity that require companies to show that no other acceptable selection alternative exists (Sovereign, 1999). As a result, many companies abandoned cognitive ability testing.

While the utility of cognitive ability testing in selection has been broadly accepted, the utility of personality testing, until relatively recently, has not. Historically, research documenting the low predictive validity and the potential for invasion of privacy based on item content has made its application as selection instruments questionable.

But due to the legal challenges associated with cognitive ability, interest in personality instruments has recently been revived. Some have suggested that pairing personality testing with cognitive ability testing may be one means to enhance validity while reducing adverse impact. Because it is very likely that some aspects of personality enhance individual ability to apply intellectual capacity while other personality traits limit its application. Hence, adding a personality to an ability test should enhance validity while reducing the adverse impact of a selection system.

Recent research studies prove this assumption to be false, by showing that the addition of a predictor producing smaller group differences (i.e., personality test) to a predictor producing higher group differences does not reduce the potential for adverse impact to the degree that is often expected.

Although the use of personality tests with measures of cognitive ability may not have the desired effects on reducing adverse impact, it appears that the addition of personality measures to measures of cognitive ability as a composite predictor results in significant incremental validity. These studies found that the validity of predictor composites was highest when alternative predictors were used in combination with cognitive ability. Though this combination of predictors resulted in the highest predictive validity, the inclusion of cognitive ability with these alternative predictors increased the potential for adverse impact.

In summary, cognitive ability testing by itself has been shown to have high levels of validity, but comes with issues relating to adverse impact. Personality tests, on the other hand, have historically been proven to have low validity due to the lack of a common understanding on what constitutes personality, and the non-standardized measures available. But a growing number of research studies show that the best way for organizations to achieve close to optimal validity and job performance prediction, is to create a predictor composite that includes a measure of cognitive ability and an additional measure such as a personality test.

Predictor validity and selection ratio

Two major factors determine the quality of newly hired employees, predictor validity and selection ratio. The predictor cut-off is a test score differentiating those passing a selection measure from those who did not. People above this score are hired or are further considered while those below it are not.

The selection ratio (SR), on the other hand is the number of job openings n divided by the number of job applicants N. This value will range between 0 and 1, reflecting the selectivity of the organization's hiring practices. When the SR is equal to 1 or greater, the use of any selection device has little meaning, but this is not often the case as there are usually more applicants than job openings. Finally, the base rate is defined by the percentage of employees thought to be performing their jobs satisfactorily following measurement.

Selection decisions

Tests designed to determine an individual's aptitude for a particular position, company or industry may be referred to as personnel assessment tools. Such tests can aid those charged with hiring personnel in both selecting individuals for hire and in placing new hires in the appropriate positions. They vary in the measurements they use and level of standardization they employ, though all are subject to error.

Predictors for selection always have less than perfect validity and scatter plots can help us to find these mistakes. The criterion cut-off is the point separating successful and unsuccessful performers according to a standard set by the hiring organization. True positives are applied those thought to succeed on the job as a result of having passed the selection test and who have, in fact, performed satisfactorily. True negatives describe those who were correctly rejected based on the measure because they would not be successful employees.

False negatives occur when people are rejected as a result of selection test failure, but would have performed well on the job anyway. Finally, false positives are applied to individuals who are selected for having passed the selection measure, but do not make successful employees. These selection errors can be minimized by increasing the validity of the predictor test.

Standards for determination of the cut-off score vary widely, but should be set to be consistent with the expectations of the relevant job. Adjusting the cut-off in either direction will automatically increase the error in the other. Thus, it is important to determine which type of error is more harmful on a case-by-case basis.

Banding is another method for setting cut-off values. Some differences in test scores are ignored as applicants whose scores fall within the same band (or, range) are selected not on the basis of individual scores, but of another factor spas to reduce adverse impact. The width of the band itself is a function of test reliability, the two being negatively correlated. Banding allows employers to ignore test scores altogether by using random selection, and many have criticized the technique for this reason.

Predicting job performance

A meta-analysis of selection methods in personnel psychology found that general mental ability was the best overall predictor of job performance and training performance.

Regarding interview procedures, there are data which put into question these tools for selecting employees. While the aim of a job interview is ostensibly to choose a candidate who will perform well in the job role, other methods of selection provide greater predictive power and often entail lower costs. Unstructured interviews are commonly used, but structured interviews tend to yield better outcomes and are considered a better practice.

Interview structure is defined as "the reduction in procedural variance across applicants, who can translate into the degree of discretion that an interviewer is allowed in conducting the interview." Structure in an interview can be compared to a typical paper and pencil test: we would not think it was fair if every test taker were given different questions and a different number of questions on an exam, or if their answers were each graded differently. Yet this is exactly what occurs in an unstructured interview; thus, a structured interview attempts to standardize this popular selection tool.

Multiple studies and meta-analyses have also been conducted to look at the relationship between organizational citizenship behaviour (OCB) and organizational performance and success. Job candidates exhibiting higher levels of helping, voice, and loyalty behaviours were generally rated as more confident, received higher salaries, and received higher salary recommendations than job candidates exhibiting these behaviours to a lesser degree. This was found to be true even candidate responses regarding task performance were taken into account. Finally, content analyses of open-ended question responses indicated selection decisions were highly sensitive to candidates with low expression of voice and helping behaviours.

CHAPTER 2

Interview of Candidate-one-on-one conversation

An interview is a conversation where questions are asked and answers are given. In common parlance, the word "interview" refers to a one-on-one conversation with one person acting in the role of the interviewer and the other in the role of the interviewee. The interviewer asks questions, the interviewee responds, with participants taking turns talking. Interviews usually involve a transfer of information from interviewee to interviewer, which is usually the primary purpose of the interview, although information transfers can happen in both directions simultaneously. One can contrast an interview which involves bi-directional communication with a one-way flow of information, such as a speech or oration.

Interviews usually take place face to face and in person, although modern communications technologies such as the Internet have enabled conversations to happen in which parties are separated geographically, such as with videoconferencing software, and of course telephone interviews can happen without visual contact. Interviews almost always involve spoken conversation between two or more parties, although in some instances a "conversation" can happen between two persons who type questions and answers back and forth. Interviews can range from unstructured or free-wheeling and open-ended conversations in which there is no predetermined plan with prearranged questions, to highly structured conversations in which specific questions occur in a specified order. They can follow diverse formats; for example, in a ladder interview, a respondent's answers typically guide subsequent interviews, with the object being to explore a respondent's subconscious motives. Typically the interviewer has some way of recording the information that is gleaned from the interviewee, often by writing with a pencil and paper, sometimes transcribing with a video or audio recorder, depending on the context and extent of information and the length of the interview. Interviews have duration in time, in the sense that the interview has a beginning and an ending.

INTERVIEWS CAN HAPPEN IN A WIDE VARIETY OF CONTEXTS:

Employment: Interviews in an employment context are typically called job interviews which describe a formal consultation for the purpose of evaluating the qualifications of the interviewee for a specific position. Interviews are seen as a useful tool in assessing qualifications. A specific type of job interview is a case interview in which the applicant is presented with a question or task or challenge, and asked to resolve the situation. Sometimes to prepare for job interviews, candidates are treated to a mock interview as a training exercise to prepare the respondent to handle questions in the subsequent 'real' interview. Sometimes the interviews happen in several waves, with the first interview sometimes being called a screening interview which is a shorter length interview, followed by more in-depth interviews later on, usually by company personnel who can ultimately hire the applicant. Technology has enabled new possibilities for interviewing; for example, video phoning technology has enabled applicants to interview for jobs despite being in different cities or countries than the interviewer.

Psychology: Psychologists use a variety of interviewing methods and techniques to try to understand and help their patients. In a psychiatric interview, a psychiatrist or psychologist or nurse asks a battery of questions to complete what is called a psychiatric assessment. Sometimes two people are interviewed by an interviewer, with one format being called couple interviews. Criminologists and detectives sometimes use cognitive interviews on eyewitnesses and victims to try to ascertain what can be recalled specifically from a crime scene, hopefully before the specific memories begin to fade in the mind.

Research: In marketing research and academic research, interviews are used in a wide variety of ways. Interviews are often used in qualitative research in which firms try to understand how consumers think. Consumer research firms sometimes use computer-assisted telephone interviewing to randomly dial phone numbers to conduct highly structured telephone interviews, with scripted questions and responses entered directly into the computer.

Journalism and Other Media: Typically, reporters covering a story in journalism conduct interviews over the phone and in person to gain information for subsequent publication. Reporters can interview political candidates on television shows. In a talk show, a radio or television "host" interviews one or more people, with the choice of topic usually being chosen by the host, sometimes for the purposes of entertainment, sometimes for informational purposes. Such interviews are often recorded and some of them can be released on an interview disc.

Other Situations: Sometimes college representatives or alumni conduct college interviews with prospective students as a way of assessing a student's suitability while offering the student a chance to learn more about a college. Some services specialize in coaching people for interviews. Government officials may conduct interviews with prospective foreign students before allowing them to study in the nation.

The Importance of the Interview Process

After the assessment and pre-screening process, the interview is your last chance to evaluate and gain critical information from a potential employee. The question is what questions you will ask and what type of answers do you desire. Beyond the experience and technical skill of the position, what are you looking for? How do you determine attitude, leadership skills, and the ability to work with your current team? How do you determine that a candidate has the personality skills and habits that you require? The interview is an art form and here are 5 responses that may help you determine whether your candidate is a Monet or a mistake.

1. **Your questions surprise the candidate consistently** – A quality candidate should anticipate roughly 80% of the questions a recruiter asks. A candidate without answers is a candidate not willing to prepare.
2. **Short answers** – Interviewees should be speaking roughly 80% of the time in an interview and every answer should be backed up by a reason for example. Short answers can potentially be a problem with work history or someone with poor people skills.

3. **The candidate without a weakness** – Everyone has flaws and the nature of the question is designed to see what the candidate is doing to improve his/her skills. The candidate with no self-awareness may even be an excellent worker, but a nightmare to work within a team environment.
4. **The enthusiastic candidate with no company knowledge** – Again, a prepared candidate will know some of the corporate history and how she/he fits into the scope of that history. Unbridled enthusiasm backed without reason indicates a lack of preparation, initiative, or intelligence.
5. **The candidate can't articulate the job and their company role** – A potential candidate should know the details of their job and an excellent candidate can discuss how his/her performance affects the company and what their job is to improve the company in the marketplace.

The interview process is not an exact science and the perfect candidate wanders into the office as often as a unicorn grazes in the open field. The greatest tool at your disposal is information and the more open-ended questions and detailed responses you gather, the greater the potential for making the best hiring decision for the company.

Importance of Interview for Employers

1. Information about job-seeking candidate

In an interview, the employer can collect complete information about the job-seeking candidate. Interview collects information about the candidate's cultural and educational background, work experience, intelligence quotient, communication skills, personality type, interests, social behaviour, etc.

2. Supplements the application blank

Due to some limitations, the job-seeking candidate cannot give his full information or details in the Application Blank for employment. However, an interviewer can collect additional relevant information of the candidate by scheduling a personal meeting with him. During meeting, interview process helps an interviewer to collect that information which is currently not available in the Application Blank. Thus, an interview supplements the Application Blank by collecting and verifying some missing information of the candidate.

3. Interview helps to select a right person

In an interview, the interviewer can see and talk to the candidates. So he can make a correct decision, whether to select or reject the candidate. Personal interview is the best method of selecting the right person for the right post.

4. Interview collects useful information

In an interview, the candidates discuss about their past work experiences, achievements, research works, etc. Interview helps an employer to collect a lot of useful information from different candidates. The employer can use this collected information to solve problems of his firm and improve efficiency.

5. Good interview increases goodwill

An interview is a public-relation tool. So, it should be conducted properly in a friendly and fearless environment. The candidates being interviewed should be treated with dignity and respect. Whether the candidate is selected or rejected, he / she should feel happy about the employer. This will boost the image of the employer. So, a good interview session always increases the goodwill of the employer.

6. Helps in promotions and transfers

A personal interview also helps an employer to evaluate his staff for promotions, transfers, etc.

Importance of Interview for Job Seekers

1. Provides employment opportunity

An interview provides an employment opportunity to the job-seeking candidate. It helps an applicant to present and communicate his views, opinions and ideas to the employer. If a candidate performs well at the interview and meets employer's expectations, then he has a good chance of getting selected for a desired post.

2. Develop confidence in candidates

Fresh job-seeking candidates (young college graduates), generally get nervous during their first few job interviews. However, after attending (facing) multiple interviews, they automatically develop a confidence in themselves. As experience builds up, they subconsciously develop skills to tackle a variety of interviews. Thus, routine interviews develop a confidence in the job-seeking candidates and boost their morale.

3. Helps candidates to accept or reject the job

The job-seeking candidate is provided with information about the job and employer. He is well-informed about the compensation (salary), perks and allowances, working condition, job security, chances of promotions and transfers, other employment benefits, if any, etc. All the doubts of the candidate are cleared by the interviewer. This helps the candidate to make a wiser career decision, whether to accept or reject the job, if offered.

4. Helps job seekers to increase contacts

When a job-seeking candidate attends an interview, he develops contacts with the interviewer and the other candidates. So, if a candidate is not selected at first job searching attempt, then these contacts sometimes help him to succeed at next job hunting attempts.

The Importance of Interview Preparation

No Matter How Confident You Feel about You're Interviewing Skills

Throughout my years as a practicing attorney and now as a legal recruiter, I have come to realise that while some people are inherently confident about their interviewing skills, most people get very nervous about interviews.

Thus, for the vast majority of us, it goes without saying that interview preparation is essential, helpful, and absolutely necessary.

But confident attorneys beware! The bottom line is that no matter how great you believe your interviewing skills are and no matter how many interviews you have "nailed" in the past, everyone benefits from proper preparation. Just as any competent attorney prepares for a client meeting, so too must the job-seeking attorney prepare for the interview.

As a helpful starting point, the following are five issues that even the most confident attorney should consider when preparing for an upcoming interview.

1. How will you answer the question "Why are you looking?"

Everyone who has ever made a lateral move has had to answer this question. It comes in many forms: "Why are you looking?"

"What brings you here today?" "So, tell me about your situation." Whatever form it takes, we all know it is coming. Yet attorneys are just as likely to struggle with this question as they are to struggle with the question that comes out of left field. Why is that?

One reason might be that the reasons for leaving a job often exist at a "gut" level. In other words, in your mind you know why you want to leave. But when it is time to articulate your reasons, the words do not always come out as smoothly as they exist in your mind.

Another reason this question can be difficult to answer is the "trying to impress" factor. Even if you have articulated your reasons for moving, chances are you have done so to a spouse, friend, or someone else you trust. But in an interview you are sitting in front of someone who is evaluating the words that come out of your mouth. Thus, you can't very well say, "I want to leave my current position because I want to bill less hours" or "I don't get along with the people in my group."

Whatever the reason, attorneys struggle with this question. The best way to ensure that you do not fall into that trap is to prepare, prepare, prepare! Put all of the reasons you want to move down on paper and work on how you can articulate those reasons to a potential employer. And make sure you practice saying them out loud. Do you sound sincere? If not, you need to go back to the pen and paper. Repeat until the words that come out of your mouth are honest, are reasonable, and demonstrate that you have given this move the thought that it deserves.

2. Do you have any nervous ticks and/or habits?

Whenever I am nervous, I twirl my hair. When I was a kid, I did it when I was having a hard time falling asleep. I did it during my SATs and every other important exam I took. I did it so much during law school that whenever I got started, one of my friends would say, "Oh, there goes Veronica, winding up her brain."

But I know myself well enough to know when I am going to launch into the hair twirling. So when I was fresh out of law school and working at the D.A.'s office, I used to wear my hair tied back whenever I was in trial. The same went for interviews — my hair was always tied back.

The moral of the story is "Know your nervous habits and control them." It sounds truly simple, but the stories I have heard of nervous ticks that sent interviews into downward spirals are endless. To name just a few: non-stop pen clicking; restless legs; talking with the hands; darting eyes; one word or expression that is used over and over again; cracking fingers; and my personal favourite, hair twirling.

These are all things that people do, and most often they don't even realize they are doing them. So know yourself and have a plan for controlling those nervous habits.

3. Be ready to listen to the questions.

To some extent, all interviews are predictable. Why are you looking to leave? What do you think makes you a good fit for our firm? What are your strengths? And so on and so forth. Now, add the fact that as attorneys we tend to think we know it all and can anticipate what comes next. The end result: even the most polished and gracious attorneys are capable of blowing interviews because they do not listen to questions before answering them.

Equally important is the need to answer the actual question that is asked. Again, as good as we are at anticipating what we will be asked, we also think we can anticipate what the interviewer wants to hear. Doing so can result in an absolute failure to actually answer the question.

The key to avoiding this is simple: listen to the question and take time to think about your answer before you start talking. Although a good interview should feel like a dialogue and not like a deposition, you should never find yourself interrupting the interviewer or talking over him or her. During your interview preparation take some time to literally visualize the interview and, in doing so, take care to visualize a scenario in which you carefully wait for the question to be asked. During the interview be extra mindful of any tendency you may have to answer the question you anticipated rather than the question that was asked.

By simply being mindful of the importance of listening, you will be much more likely to actually listen and answer the question that is asked.

4. What will you wear?

As law firms and companies across the country shift from ultra-conservative to business casual, the unavoidable temptation is to question the need for formal interview attire.

Don't do it. Unless the hiring contact for the firm specifically instructs the attorney-candidate to wear anything other than a conservative suit, all traditional rules apply when it comes to interview attire. Even if the person who interviews you is in jeans and a polo, remember that you are the one asking to be hired.

When it comes to interview preparation, I highly recommend planning what you are going to wear so that you are not scrambling on the day of the interview. Even if you have 20 navy blue suits in your closet, identify the one you plan to wear and make sure it is dry-cleaned and lint-free. When in doubt, dress as if you are appearing before the most conservative judge in your district.

5. *Do your homework!*

Making a connection with your interviewer is crucial. However, many people think that if they are "good with people," the connection will happen naturally. While having natural rapport with people is a key factor, there is much more than that to a successful interview. Today's job market is highly competitive, and as much as interviewers want to know that you are easy to get along with, they also want to know that you have given serious thought to your move and, more importantly, to their firm.

Thus, beyond thinking of how you will answer common interview questions and what you will wear, you must take the time to gather information that will enable you to convey interest in the particular opportunity before you.

Know your interviewer; know the firm; and know what questions you are going to ask about the firm and the practice you seek to join.

Remember: interview preparation is absolutely essential in today's job market. Do not allow yourself to fall into the trap of thinking you can "wing" it — your interviewer will know that you have done so and will undoubtedly conclude that you are not truly invested in your job search. By taking the time to think about the five issues presented here, you will know that you have covered the essentials of interview preparation, and that alone will be a tremendous confidence booster.

CHAPTER 3

Developing Your Personal Themes

Too many job seekers jump right into a full-scale job search without much advance preparation other than putting together a resume. A serious mistake! Although your resume may get you job interviews, to win job offers, you must prepare yourself further. It's vitally important to distinguish yourself in some positive way from other candidates vying for the same position. One way of accomplishing this is by developing several themes that you continually refer to throughout the job interview. This enables you to emphasize your strongest points and ensures that you'll leave a positive impression in the recruiter's mind.

DEVELOPING YOUR PERSONAL THEMES FOR THE JOB INTERVIEW

There are twelve types of information recruiters seek in a typical job interview. Knowing what these points are, and being able to discuss readily how each point relates to you, will make you better prepared and more in control of the inter viewing process. Think of your twelve themes as sales mes sages. Each is designed to showcase your best skills and qualifications. Together, they make up a twelve-point strategy that will enable you to sell your qualifications in virtually any interview situation.

Read through the following twelve topics. Develop a personalized approach to each and practice talking about it. Think of specific examples in your background that correspond to each topic. You can't possibly be prepared for every situation, but once you've developed your twelve key messages, you'll be able to apply them to almost any interview question you face.

Next, turn to chapter 4 to review common interview questions relating to each of the twelve themes. Try to answer each question aloud; incorporating the themes you've developed.

Then evaluate your progress. You may discover that you need more practice in order to become comfortable discussing the topics in a clear and concise manner. Nothing that you say for the first time will come out the way you like. Practice aloud delivering your twelve key messages until the words come easily in an organized yet comfortable, conversational way.

1. Passion for the Business

Ask yourself, "Why am I interested in working in this field in this industry?" Do you feel a passion for the business? Why it is so? Give specific examples of the things that excite you.

These could be anything from enjoying the challenge of meeting increasingly higher sales goals, to a sense of satisfaction derived from developing a product from the creation stage to final production. Offer personal experience where possible.

2. Motivation and Purpose

Interviewers will want to know why you want to work for their particular company. Ask yourself, "Why do I want this interview?" Don't simply repeat your resume and employment history. What's the most compelling case you can make to prove your interest? Have you used the company's products or talked to its customers or competitors? (Refer to the section that follows, "Researching Potential Employers," to learn how you can locate this kind of information about companies you're interested in.)

3. Skills and Experience

Consider your key skills and how you'll use them in this job. Avoid clichés and generalities; instead, offer specific evidence. Think about your weaknesses and how you can minimize and balance them with your strengths. Try to describe yourself as objectively as possible. Avoid sounding arrogant or defensive.

4. Diligence and Professionalism

Describe your professional character, including thoroughness, diligence, and accountability. Give proof that you persevere to see important projects through, and that you achieve desired results.

Demonstrate how you gather resources, how you predict obstacles, and how you manage stress.

5. *Creativity and Leadership*

You please offer proof of your effectiveness, including creativity, initiative, resourcefulness, and leadership. What examples can you provide for each? Focus on how you overcome problems, how you take advantage of opportunities that might otherwise be overlooked, and how you rally the support of others to accomplish goals.

6. *Compatibility with the Job*

Discuss your specific qualifications for the job. How well do they fit the requirements of the position? Your answer should describe both positive and negative aspects of recent jobs, without dwelling on the negatives. Conclude by focusing on what you're seeking in your next job. Keep in mind that your response should match closely the position you're applying for.

7. *Personality and Cultural Compatibility*

Consider your personality on the job. How do you fit in with other types of personalities? What types of people would enjoy working with you for hours at a time? How would the company's customers or clients react to you? Your goal is to develop responses that make the interviewer feel confident there won't be any surprises about your personality on the job.

8. *Management Style and Interpersonal Skills*

Talk about the management style and the interpersonal skills you use with peer groups and leaders. Focus on how you work rather than on what type of work you do well. What kind of boss, colleague, and employee will you be? Give personal or popular examples of leaders you believe are effective.

Why are those people able to accomplish so much?

9. *Problem-Solving Ability*

Offer proof, with examples, of your problem-solving ability. How have you resolved difficult issues in the past? Are you practical in how you apply technical skills? Are you realistic?

Focus on real issues, on logical value-added solutions, on practical outcomes of your work, and on realistic measures of judging these outcomes.

10. Accomplishments

Think about your initiative and accomplishments. Offer examples in which you've delivered more than what was expected. Don't give long descriptions of situations; instead, focus your answer on the action you took and the positive results you obtained. If you were hired, what situations would you handle especially well? What can you contribute to the organization?

11. Career Aspirations

Tailor your aspirations to the realities of this particular job and its career path. Avoid listing job titles or offering unrealistic performance deadlines. Instead, reiterate the skills and strengths you want to develop further. Do you want cross functional experience, a larger budget, or more supervisory responsibility? Why would you be effective with that additional experience?

12. Personal Interests and Hobbies

Do you have a balanced lifestyle? Is your personality reflected in the type of job you choose as well as in the outside activities you pursue? Are your personal and career interests compatible? The interviewer will also be interested in your community involvement. How commendably would you reflect the company's image?

After you feel comfortable with your twelve sales messages, develop them in a brief summary. This is a useful tool that you can use effectively at the end of the interview, when the interviewer says something like "Is there anything else you'd like to tell me?" Never let an interview end without summarizing your twelve key messages.

The Sixty-Second Pitch

Another good preparation technique is the sixty-second pitch.

Approximately one week after you've sent your resume to a key decision maker, you should follow up with a phone call.

Don't simply ask if your resume has been received—this can be frustrating to employers who are inundated with hundreds of resumes. A better approach is to state that you've sent your resume and explain, in sixty seconds or less, why you think you're the best candidate for the position. Your sixty-second pitch should be a clear and concise summary of yourself, including three important elements:

- What kind of work you do (or want to do)

- What your strongest skills and accomplishments are
- What kind of position you're seeking

If you're invited to an interview after you've pitched yourself to the hiring manager, great! If not, don't let it end there!

Ask if there are any particular qualifications that he or she is looking for in a candidate. Is there anything else you can do or any additional information that you can send (writing samples, clippings, or portfolio) to help the hiring manager make a decision? Even if the person says no, that your resume is sufficient, he or she may be impressed by your interest and enthusiasm.

If you haven't already done so, specifically ask the employer if he or she would have a few minutes to meet with you. If that doesn't work, ask if that person knows anyone who might be interested in speaking to someone with your qualifications. If you're unable to arrange an interview or to get a referral, ask the employer if he or she would mind if you called back in a month or so. The goal is to get a positive response from the phone call—whether it's an interview or simply a scrap of job-hunting advice. Don't give up too easily, but be professional and courteous at all times.

Researching Potential Employers

There are two good reasons why you should set aside sometime early in your job search to research companies in your field of interest. First, it's a great way to locate potential employers. Second, it's an effective way to learn more about particular companies you're considering working for.

Researching potential employers can be time-consuming, but it's well worth the effort. To use your time effectively, however, you should divide your research into two distinct phases. The first phase should involve gathering only basic information about many different companies, including:

- Company name, address, phone and fax numbers
- Names and job titles of key contacts
- Whether the company is privately or publicly held
- Products and/or services
- Year of incorporation
- Number of employees

The second phase of research begins as you start to schedule job interviews. This involves gathering more detailed information about each company you're interviewing with.

Your goal is to be able to walk into an interview knowing the organization inside and out. You need to know the company's products, types of customers, subsidiaries, parent company, principal locations, rank in the industry, sales and profit trends, type of ownership, size, current plans, principal competitors and their relative performance, and much more

Incorporating this knowledge into your discussions is certain to impress the toughest of interviewers and will distinguish you from the competition. The more time you spend on this phase, the better prepared you'll be. Even if you feel extremely pressed for time, you should set aside at least twelve hours for preinterview research.

Where to Look

To find the information you need, you'll have to dig into every resource you can find. Libraries are a fantastic source of both publicized and hidden job opportunities. Most have a vast array of resources, including major newspapers like the

New York Times and the Wall Street Journal and trade journals like Advertising Age and Publishers Weekly. To identify publications in your field of interest, consult the Encyclopaedia of Business Information Sources or Predicates F&S Index.

There are a number of other resources you can use to find listings of companies, most of which can also be found at your local library. Ask the reference librarian to help you locate the many directories that list basic information about companies in your field of interest. Be sure not to overlook these great tools:

The Job Bank series published by Adams Media Corporation is a good place to start. Each book in the series is a regional employment guide covering a specific metropolitan area. The Boston Job Bank, for example, includes thousands of employers in Massachusetts.

Unlike most other industry guides, who cost hundreds of dollars and may be found only at libraries, the local Job Bank books cost only $16.95 and can be purchased wherever books are sold.

Dun and Bradstreet's Million Dollar Directory lists approximately 160,000 companies that are both publicly and privately held and is updated annually.

Standard & Poor's Register of Corporations lists fewer companies than the Million Dollar Directory (about 45,000) but provides valuable biographical information on thousands of company officials.

Corporate Technology Directory (Corporate Technology Information Services) focuses on the products of approximately 35,000 companies. This is a great resource for job seekers interested in high-tech industries, including computers, biotechnology, environmental engineering, chemical and pharmaceutical, and transportation.

Personnel Executives Contact book (Gale Research) lists key personnel and other contacts at 30,000 publicly and privately held companies and government agencies.

The National Job Bank (Adams Media Corporation) lists key contacts at over 21,000 small and large companies. It includes information on common positions filled and educational backgrounds desired and is updated annually.

Directory of Human Resources Executives (Hunt-Scanlon) names human-resource executives and provides information on number of employees and area of specialization of 5,000 public and private companies.

Directory of Corporate Affiliations (National Register) is one of the few places where you can find information on a company's divisions and subsidiaries. This particular book lists information on approximately 4,000 parent companies.

Also, don't overlook the countless industry-specific directories that are available, such as The Job Bank Guide to Computer & High-Tech Companies, The Job Bank Guide to Health Care Companies, Dunn's Directory of Service Companies, Martindale-Hubbell Law Directory, and Standard Directory of Advertisers.

These are terrific places to find potential employers and often include information on professional associations and industry trends.

Many of these resources can also be found on CD-ROM at your library. These "books on disk" are easy to use and can save you a lot of time. They are often attached to printers, so you can print the information you need. Usually, libraries will provide free access to CD-ROM databases.

Your local library is not the only place to look for valuable company information. Why not go straight to the source? Call the investor-relations departments of companies you're interested in and request their annual report. (This approach will generally work only with larger companies.) Call the sales office or PR office of the parent company to get a copy of any literature distributed to consumers, including product literature, recent press releases, or even annual reports (for public companies). If the company is public, call a stockbroker and ask for additional information to supplement what's already in your file. If the firm has a human-resources department, ask for a recruitment package or any other information available to job seekers. If you're interested in a smaller company that doesn't have a human-resources department or publish annual reports, don't panic! Most companies have brochures or catalogs of their products or services that they'll send to you upon request. If possible, speak to someone at the firm before the interview. If you can't do this, speak to someone at a competing firm. The more time you spend the better.

Use all of your research to develop educated, informed opinions. You'll be better prepared to exchange ideas, create interesting conversation, and make a positive impression on the interviewer.

The Informational Interview

Particularly if you're an entry-level job seeker or a career change, you should consider conducting at least one informational interview. An informational interview is simply a meet ing that you arrange to talk to someone in a field, industry, or company that interests you. With the help of this kind of interview, you can prepare for a real job interview in several ways, including:

- Examining your compatibility with the company by comparing the realities of the field (skills required, working conditions, schedules, and common traits of people you meet) to your own personal interests
- Finding out how people in a particular business, Indus try, or job view their roles and the growth opportunities in their businesses
- Conducting primary research on companies and industries
- Gaining insight into the kinds of topics your potential interviewers will be concerned about and the methods for interviewing
- Getting feedback on your relative strengths and weaknesses as a potential job candidate
- Becoming comfortable talking to people in the industry and learning the industry jargon
- Building your network, which can lead to further valuable information and opportunities?

To set up an informational appointment, request a meeting with someone who has at least several years' experience working in your field of interest. Your goal is to learn how that person got into the business, what he or she likes about it, and what kind of advice someone with experience might pass on to someone who's interested in entering the field

Tell your contact right away that you'd like to learn more about the industry or company, and that you'll be the one asking all the questions. Most people won't feel threatened (especially if you assure them you're not asking them for a job) and will usually be inclined to help you.

If you tell a contact that all you want is advice, though, make sure you mean it. Never approach an informational interview as though it were a job interview—just stick to gathering information and leads and see what happens. Also, unless specifically requested to do so, sending your resume to someone you'd like to meet for an informational interview will probably give the wrong impression.

Conducting Informational Interviews

Now that you've scheduled an informational interview, make sure you're prepared to take the lead. After all, you're the one doing the interviewing—not vice versa. Prepare a list of ten to twenty questions, such as:

- How did you get started in this business?
- What experience helped you to be prepared and qualified for this job? (How did you get to this point in your career?)
- What do you believe is the ideal education and background?
- What are your primary responsibilities in your current job?
- What do you like most about your job, your company, and your industry?
- What do you dislike most about them?
- What's been your greatest challenge?

If you could work with anybody in this field, whom would you want to work with?

- Five years out, what are your career goals?
- What are typical career path options from here?
- If you could change something about your career path, what would you change?
- What are the most valuable skills to have in this field?

- What specific experiences helped you build these skills?
- What opportunities do you see in this business?
- Why did you want this job?
- What would you say are the current career opportunities for someone with my qualifications in the industry?
- If you were in the job market tomorrow, how would you get started? What would you do?
- What are the basic requirements for an entry-level position in the industry?
- What do you consider a must-read list in your field?
- Where do you see the industry heading in the near future?
- Is there a trade association that might aid me in my job search?
- What things impress you when you interview candidates for positions in this field?
- What are turnoffs when you interview candidates?
- What critical questions should I expect to be asked in a job interview?
- What advice would you give to someone looking for a job in the industry?
- Is there anything else I should know about the industry?
- Do you know of anyone who might be looking for someone with my qualifications?
- Is there anything you think I should've brought up (but didn't) that should be a consideration? (What have I missed in this line of questioning?)

Always end by thanking the person and promising to follow up on any important leads he or she has provided and to let the person know how things turn out. You should also send a thank-you note within one or two days of the informational interview.

Follow up periodically with everyone in your network—even after you get a job. Once you develop a network, it's important not to lose those contacts. You want to translate your informational network into a support network and maintain it throughout your career.

Preparing for Telephone Interviews

Telephone screening interviews are becoming more common place because companies want to reduce their hiring costs by avoiding travel at screening stages in interviews. Using phone interviews, recruiters can quickly weed out most candidates and decide on the best candidates to pursue—that is, to invite for a face-to-face interview. This is when developing a sixty second pitch can also come in handy.

Here's why planning for a telephone interview is so important: unlike a planned first interview, for which you have done all the preparation already discussed, a telephone interview can come at any time and from any company. Also, once you begin to network, a phone interview may result when all you expected was possible leads. Sometimes recruiters will call to schedule an interview at a later time, but more often they'll call hoping to interview you on the spot.

Here are some general tips for handling a phone interview:

- If you feel unprepared or uncomfortable with your phone skills, practice with a friend. Role-play and ask a friend to question you over the phone. Also, you can make good use of your answering machine, here; call when you're away from home and leave yourself a message emphasizing one of your themes. When you get home, listen to how you sound; listen to your voice pat tern (enthusiasm, highs/lows, pauses, and so on). Also listen to the content—was your message clear and direct? Keep practicing until you're comfortable with the results.
- Always be prepared, with your twelve themes ready to go. The basic guidelines of a screening interview apply here as well.
- Keeps a copy of your resume by the phone, along with a list of key words representing the themes you think are relevant to the industry or job category you're pursuing?
- You can't count on clues from an interviewer's body language, eye contact, or other such signs. You'll have to pay close attention, instead, to their voice pattern, and you must use your own voice—simple, direct, enthusiastic responses—to keep the conversation interesting and easy to follow.
- Listen very carefully and maintain your highest level of concentration. Have a phone set up where you can sit more or less as you'd sit for an interview. Keep a pen and some paper near the phone, along with your resume and notes. Take very careful notes about what you're asked and what seemed most

critical to the recruiter. (This information will help you follow up later with a letter.)

- Avoid long pauses; provide quick summaries of your key themes or points with clear examples of how you've made positive contributions where you've been and how you could contribute to this company.
- Make sure you get the name (spelled correctly), number, and address of the person who called.
- Reaffirm your interest—if you're interested after this first round. Find out what happens next and what you can do to make yourself competitive. Follow up with a thank-you note, just as you would for a screening interview. Your goal is to get face-to-face in the next round.

Collecting References

At some point before you start interviewing, you'll need to prepare a list of three to five references. Unless you're new to the workforce, at least two of these should be professional references from previous employers or close business associates. Other potential sources of references include teachers, professors, volunteer committee heads, and friends who are well respected in business circles. Don't list family members as references.

Be sure to ask people for their permission before you cite them as references. If they agree, be sure you have their job title, the name of the company where they work, and their work address and phone number. Then prepare a neat, typed list of your reference contacts with your name at the top of the page. You should make several copies and have them on hand during your job interviews. Don't make the mistake of listing your references on your resume, as this is commonly considered inappropriate and unprofessional.

Don't forget to send each of your references a thank-you note when your job search is over. Proper etiquette aside, this practice will help keep your contacts current. You never know when you might need their help again sometime down the road.

CHAPTER 4

Interacting effectively with the interviewer

By now, you've probably spent a great deal of time preparing. However, you must not let your practice and preparation become a disadvantage. Once the interview begins, you must focus on interacting effectively with the interviewer—as opposed to trying to recall precisely the responses you practiced earlier. If you've prepared adequately for the interview, your conduct and responses should effortlessly convey to the interviewer the image you want to project.

It's important for you to know that the interviewer's decision about whether or not you'll be invited back for an additional interview will probably be influenced by your attitude and personality as much as by your qualifications. So although preparation is important, your performance during an interview can make an even greater difference. Generally, you should try to stress the following qualities in your choice of words, your tone of voice, and your body language:

- Capability
- Confidence
- Dependability
- Easygoing manner
- Enthusiasm
- Flexibility
- Resourcefulness
- Strong work ethic

A word of caution: Don't concentrate too much on trying to project the perfect image. Just try to relax, visualize yourself as smooth and confident, and you'll almost certainly do well.

Dressing for Success

How important is proper dress for a job interview? Although the final selection of a job candidate will rarely be determined by dress, first-round candidates are often eliminated because they've dressed inappropriately This is not to say you should invest in a new wardrobe; just be sure that you're able to put together an adequate interview outfit. A good rule of thumb is to dress for a position just above the one you're applying for. Men should wear a clean, conservative, two-piece suit; a white shirt; and a silk tie. Lace-up wing tips are your best bet for shoes. This is the basic corporate wardrobe; however, in some industries, a quality jacket, pants, shirt, and tie are fine.

But if you're not sure what dress is appropriate at a certain firm, play it safe and opt for a two-piece suit. A man should always wear a jacket and tie to an interview—even if everyone else in the office is in shirt sleeves. Dressing this way shows you're taking the interview seriously and treating the company with respect.

For women, a professional-looking dress or suit with low heeled shoes makes the best impression. In more conservative industries, like law or banking, a suit's probably your best choice. However, some hiring managers in creative industries, like advertising or publishing, look for a more informal, stylish look that reflects the applicant's individuality. Use your best judgment and wear whatever is both professional and comfortable for you. However, be sure to avoid excess jewelry or makeup.

Impeccable personal grooming is even more important than finding the perfect outfit. Be sure that your clothes are clean, pressed, and well fitting, and that your shoes are polished. Hair should be neat and business like, and your nails should be clean and trimmed. Both men and women are advised to skip the cologne or perfume—you never know if the person interviewing you will be violently allergic to the cologne you're wearing.

Timing Is Everything

Although it may seem hard to believe, many job seekers arrive late for interviews. This is easy enough to do—you might simply take a little unplanned extra time to prepare for your interview or underestimate how long it will take to get to the interview location. Don't let yourself make this fatal mistake!

Allow plenty of time to get ready for, and to travel to, your job interview. You shouldn't arrive at the interviewer's office more than ten minutes in advance. However, if you're driving across town, allowing yourself an extra ten minutes probably isn't enough. Try to get to the location at least thirty minutes early; you can then spend twenty minutes in a nearby coffee shop or take a walk around the building. Interviews are important enough to build in a little extra time. Here's another tip: If you've never been to the interview location, visit it the day before so you know exactly how to get there, how to access the building, and where to park.

Sometimes the interviewer will be running behind schedule. Don't be upset: be sympathetic. Interviewers are often pressured to see a lot of candidates and to fill a demanding position quickly. So be sure to come to your interview with good reading material to keep yourself occupied and relaxed.

What to Have on Hand

A briefcase or leather-bound folder, if you have one, will help complete the professional, polished look you want to achieve.

Women should avoid carrying a purse if they plan on carrying a briefcase—it may detract from a professional image. And don't forget to wear a watch!

Before leaving for the interview, be sure that you have good directions and the phone numbers and names of the people you'll be meeting with. You should also bring the following items with you to the interview:

- Several unfolded copies of your resume and cover letter
- A note pad and pen (for taking notes during the interview)
- A list of professional references
- Examples of your work, such as writing samples or clippings (taking care that these don't breach the confidentiality of previous employers)

Body Language

The first minutes of the interview are the most important. A recruiter begins sizing up your potential the instant you walk into the room. If you make a bad impression from the start, you may be ruled out immediately, and the interviewer may pay little attention to your performance during the rest of the interview. An excellent initial impression, on the other hand, will put a favourable glow on everything else you say during the rest of the interview—and could well encourage the recruiter to ask less demanding questions.

How can you ensure that you make a terrific first impression? The easiest answer is to be sure you're dressed well.

When the recruiter meets you, he or she will notice your clothes and grooming first. Nothing other than impeccable grooming is acceptable. Your attire must be professional and squeaky clean.

Your body language will also speak volumes, even before you and the interviewer exchange a word. Any recruiter will unconsciously pick up on and react to the subtle signals of body language. Here are some important things to think about:

- Do you smile when you meet?
- Do you make just enough eye contact without staring at the recruiter?
- Do you walk into the office with a self-assured and confident stride?
- Do you shake hands firmly?
- Are your briefcase, note pad, and coat in your left hand, or do you have to juggle them around in order to shake hands?
- Do your eyes travel naturally to and from the recruiter's face as you begin to talk?
- Do you remember the recruiter's name and pronounce it with confidence?
- Do you make small talk easily, or do you act formal and reserved, as though under attack?

Its human nature to judge people by that first impression, so make sure yours is a good one. But most of all, try to be you.

Overcoming Nervousness

As if formulating solid answers to interview questions isn't tough enough, you'll also have to overcome a quite natural, inevitable nervousness. Most employers won't think less of a job candidate for a bit of nervous behaviour—but they will pay close attention to how you hold up under pressure.

Displaying excessive nervousness can easily eliminate you from further consideration.

One good way to overcome preinterview jitters is to exercise positive thinking. If you're feeling nervous about an upcoming interview, imagine in detail what the experience will be like: Think of what you'll say, the questions you'll be asked, and how you'll answer them. Picture yourself responding calmly, effectively, and in a controlled manner. This type of mental rehearsing won't guarantee success, but it should help you feel more optimistic and self-confident, which will undoubtedly enhance your final presentation.

Above all, you should practice interviewing as much as you can. You'll become more confident and your answers will become more polished with each interview you have.

The Importance of Body Language in a Group Discussion or Personal Interview

The above statement applies to all conversations in general. However, it holds prime importance in the context of a group discussion or interview. A large number of MBA aspirants prepare passionately for important GD topics and appropriate answers to some of the common interview questions. However, shocking as it may be, what you speak during the procedure carries only a part of the entire weightage that the process holds.

What interviewers and GD panel members use to evaluate your personality is more than the words you speak. The panel members and interviewers keenly observe the body language of the candidates. What they perceive about your personality can easily make or break your chances of getting admission in a B-school. Therefore, it is very important for every candidate to portray a positive body language to be able to create a good impression in the interview.

Read on to know more about the right attitude and body language that can be helpful in cracking the MBA admission procedure at the B-school of your choice.

Importance of Positive Body Language

To understand the importance of positive body language, candidates must understand that it is not just the mouth that speaks but the entire body acts as an instrument of speech. So, you must first understand how your body speaks and then learn to manage and control the non-verbal messages that you send across to your audience.

Demonstrating a positive body language is important as interviewers pay attention to the slightest details of your postures and gestures during the interview. Experts advise that you must know how to use your body to effectively enhance your verbal message. Leaning forward slightly towards the group during the Group Discussion and the interviewer during the Personal Interview would go on to show that you are interested. Giving listening cues such as nodding whenever a fellow aspirant/interviewer makes an important point shows your engagement in the process.

On the other hand, gestures such as scratching your head, repeatedly crossing and uncrossing the legs or touching your face are all instances of a nervous body language. These actions must be avoided by the candidates to be able to make a positive impact on the panel members.

Body Language: Things to Consider

Shake Hands Properly

The handshake is a courteous way to acknowledge your interviewer but you should not take initiative to shake hands. Let the interviewer shake hands with you as this is the right way to proceed in an interview. The handshake is the first unspoken assessment of your personality. So, make every effort to impress your interviewer with a confident and firm handshake. Some candidates may shake hands too firmly while others might engage in too limp a handshake. The former might indicate aggressiveness and dominating attitude while the latter one is a sign of weak personality—both of which aren't good. A proper handshake is firm to the right extent, gives the right kind of contact for an appropriate duration. With a smile and good eye contact, it becomes a good one.

Smile

A smiling face portrays exuberance and eagerness and it is a good way to impress your interviewers and the panel members of the group discussion. A smiling and happy demeanour shows that you are really happy to be where you are. But, don't go overboard with it as an artificial or oversized smile can have the wrong effect. An experienced interviewer will immediately know if you are acting or forcing the smile in a certain way. It is good to smile sometimes when you actually mean it during the interview and group discussion rather than grinning constantly without any reason.

Be Careful Of Personal Space

Individual cultures and faiths in the different candidates who come for admission to the MBA program tend to make them different in all aspects including an appropriate personal space. Some people may feel comfortable speaking only inches from the other person while others may need a decent space. When sitting in a group discussion, you must ensure that you respect the personal space that the candidate sitting beside you. Similarly, when in front of your interviewer, be careful of how far or close you sit.

Be Expressive and Open

Your physical gestures must be expressive and open. You must try to engage your interviewer by gesturing positively such as keeping your palms straight and open which demonstrates honesty. You should never bang your hand on the table and always avoid pointing fingers to make a point during the group discussion and personal interview. These negative physical gestures would not go well with your interviewing panel and should be strictly avoided.

Demonstrate Inquisitiveness

Maintaining an eye contact and nodding your head are the best ways to show your eagerness or interest in an interview as well as the group discussion. The panel will appreciate that you are actively engaged in the discussion and paying attention to what the others are saying. Lack of eye contact and other listening cues would suggest your disinterest in the interview and weaken your chances to succeed.

Body Language: Things You Should Avoid

Looking Disinterested

Physical gestures such as rubbing the back of the head, touching the nose or hair would signal your disinterest in the interview. Therefore, these actions should be avoided in spite of the bouts of nervousness and stress that you might be experiencing before the interview. Try to sit straight confidently without leaning too forward or bending too backwards during both the group discussion and interview.

Signalling Nervousness

Some candidates may unknowingly grab their folder or bag too tightly or may constantly touch and wipe their face in front of the interviewer. Other gestures such as tapping the fingers, biting or licking the lips, frowning, adjusting hair or clothing again and again must also be avoided for a positive impression on the panel members. These gestures signal the candidate's nervousness even though he may be trying hard to hide it. The interviewers are smarter and more experienced than you are, so, they can easily perceive gestures that portray anxiety or nervousness. So, try to remain calm and relaxed and do not make unnecessary movements. While being nervous is natural and many interviewers may not find it negative, it will still increase your inhibitions and degrade your performance.

Getting Too Relaxed

Lounging with your arms and legs dangling would suggest you are getting too relaxed for the group discussion and interview. Similarly, crossed feet and completely stretched out legs also demonstrate you are very relaxed for the group discussion and this may also be taken for over confidence on your part. Therefore, you should try to show some seriousness by listening attentively and speaking meaningfully without making any carefree gestures that undermine your intent and eagerness in the selection procedure.

Becoming Defensive

Crossing your arms in front of the interviewer can be perceived as being defensive. It might also suggest that according to you, whatever you are saying is correct and you do not want to accommodate someone else's views or opinions at all. Therefore, it is advised not to cross your arms during the interview and discussion processes. Instead, sit upright with your arms rested on your thighs to cut out a confident picture.

It might be easy to prepare for the group discussion and the verbal component of the personal interview by studying hard and being well versed with the latest happenings of the world. But candidates should understand that portraying a positive body language is as important as speaking and performing well in the group discussion and personal interview. It is not just about questions and their right answers, but about participating in the selection processes with a favourable body language. Show them that you have the power of expression in you!

Personal interviews represent a bridge that candidates must cross to move from job seeker to new hire. However, many interviewees fail to appreciate personal interviews as a pre-acceptance tool that can help them avoid making a career mistake. According to Dr. Ann Howard, past president of the Society for Industrial and Organizational Psychology, interviews help the candidate and employer make an informed, mutually beneficial employment choice. Candidates who understand both sides of the interviewing process stand to have a more successful job search.

Company Perspective

Human resource departments approach recruitment with a keen awareness of the financial side of employment: A company's workforce represents its largest or second largest expense. A bad hire, notes Illinois-based HR specialist RGL Consultants, can cost as much as 150 percent of the new employee's annual compensation. Intangible costs of picking the wrong candidate — lost productivity, a drop in morale, reduced customer service — add to HR's concern. Successful hiring requires more than discovering the ideal resume; it needs conversations — personal interviews — to assess a candidate's capabilities and his compatibility, or fit, with the organization's culture.

Fit

Cultural fit reflects the working environment: how employees dress, comport themselves, interact with each other and their supervisors, make decisions and treat customers. Dr. Charles Handler, a recognized thought leader in talent assessment, dubs a worker's compatibility to company culture as "person-organization fit." For the organization, a sound P-O fit translates into employee engagement, productivity, low absenteeism and reduced turnover. For the candidate, it means the difference between enjoying a job and being miserable at work. Personal interviews let both parties judge P-O fit. HR may schedule interviews with other staff members for opinions on how the candidate's personality and work-style match the organization. The candidate can use these conversations to learn more about the employer and the position as well as to visualize how he might forge working relationships with would-be colleagues. Appearance, tone of voice and body language give everyone involved clues about cultural fit.

Candidate Perspective

An interview invitation means that something in a job-seekers credentials triggered curiosity about him as a solution to the organization's needs. The personal interview gives him an opportunity to learn the exact nature of those needs and sell his ability to fill them while discovering more about the position and the organization. Spending time under a potential employer's roof gives a glimpse into life on the job. Watching employees at work provides insight about camaraderie that may or may not correspond with candidate desires. Touring the facilities sheds light on company stability, pride and worker respect.

Preparation

Before interviewing, candidate should prepare questions as they research the company. According to the career resources website Pro Net, asking questions during an interview is half information-gathering and half showcasing competence. Questions related to the department's role in the organization, the parameters and challenges faced, why the position is open, training, possibilities for promotion, performance evaluation, benefits, compensation and work style will reveal pertinent information unavailable from published sources. Inquiring about recent changes the department has undergone, competition, how the company defines success, management's leadership style and how the department supports the organization's mission statement can help the candidate glean valuable information about the company's stability and prospects. As author and change management specialist Gregg Stocker notes, the company needs to sell itself as an employer of choice. Candidate questions help them do that.

The Value or Importance of a Job Interview

Job interviews can be a nerve-wracking experience for the applicant and a time-consuming exercise for the hiring company. However, they play a key role in determining whether the company and candidate will make an effective match. As such, the interviewing process provides a great deal of value for the company and candidate alike.

Making an Impression

Though the candidate's resume, cover letter and job application give interviewers an overview of her background and skills, the interview may be the best chance the candidate has to make a favorable impression. For better or worse, the candidate's physical appearance and ability to handle herself during the questioning will leave a lasting impression and play a vital role in the interviewer's decision-making process. The interviewer also uses the process to assess the candidate's personality to determine if she would be a good fit for the organization.

Exchanging Information

The job interview serves as a two-way street for the exchange of information. The interviewer has the opportunity to learn more about the candidate's background and can also impart more in-depth information about the company and the various duties the job entails. The candidate also has the chance to ask questions to gain additional insight regarding the expectations of the job and to get a better feel for the organization's culture.

Selling Opportunity

The interview provides a selling opportunity for the organization as well as the candidate. The interviewer can highlight the positive aspects of working for the company, such as how plans for growth can lead to future opportunities or how the company is recognized as an industry leader. Candidates can expand upon their skills and positive personal attributes to demonstrate how they can help the company achieve its short-term and long-term objectives.

Narrowing the Field

In situations where companies receive a heavy volume of applicants for a job opening, interviews are a valuable tool for narrowing the field. In particular, a round of preliminary interviews helps the company to weed out unsuitable candidates so it can then pay closer attention to the "cream of the crop" in subsequent interviews. For job seekers fortunate enough to possess skills that are in great demand, they can use the interview process to help determine which company would ultimately be the best fit.

Explanation about the Importance of Job Interviews

A job interviews enable a company to learn more about an applicant, while the candidate has the opportunity to become familiar with the demands of a given position. The process allows both parties to exchange information, ask questions and evaluate the potential for establishing a professional working relationship. Both parties have an opportunity to get a "feel" for one another other and determine if the chemistry is right

Learn the Corporate Dynamic

A thorough understanding of the job opening and the ability to articulate what you bring to the position is a major asset. Also, the manner in which the employer approaches the interview will offer insight into the day-to-day realities of the work place. If the interview is light, conversational and includes a good back-and-forth discussion, that's an indication that the workplace is relaxed. If the interview feels formal or impersonal, it's likely to be a reflection of a more conservative culture.

Sell Your Abilities

The interview gives the employer its first impression of you and provides you with a crucial opportunity to "sell" yourself. The manner in which you present yourself often determines if you are offered the job. You want to establish yourself as a highly competent individual who is well suited for the position — as well as a competitive salary. The interview also sets the stage for your long-term relationship with the company, establishing your potential for advancement.

Gauge Career Potential

If you have a long-term career plan, the interview is your opportunity to assess if the employer provides the potential for professional development. When discussing long-range goals, the employer can also get a better idea of your objectives, and you can gauge if there's room for significant growth. Ask about mentoring opportunities, the company's policy toward promoting from within, and inquire about upper-level positions to which you might one day ascend.

Determine Earning Power

Many employers don't discuss salary and benefits until the interview stage. After establishing your qualifications, this is an opportunity to discuss compensation, pay increase schedules, retirement plans and perks. You can also inquire if profit-sharing and bonus programs are in place, and discuss your ultimate earning potential.

Meet Potential Colleagues

Some interview formats, especially panel interviews, afford the opportunity to meet potential colleagues. This is especially true in second and third-round meetings when interviewers attempt to assess how well you will fit in with the existing team. Talking to these staffers can help you determine if your personalities will mesh. Ask employees what they enjoy most about their jobs as well as what they see as the most challenging aspects. Take note of how they interact with each other.

CHAPTER 5

Navigating the Dynamics of Interview Conversation

All your preparation should be evident when the conversation gets going. Make sure your tone remains conversational; don't let the interview turn into an interrogation. Start by thanking the interviewer for the opportunity to talk with him or her and explain up front why you're interested in the position. Be ready to answer and to ask questions, including occasionally asking the interviewer for his or her own perspective on a subject.

After small talk, the interviewer may well begin by telling you about the company, the division, the department, or perhaps the position. Because of your detailed research, information about the company should be already familiar to you. The interviewer will probably like nothing better than to avoid this regurgitation of company history, so if you can do so tactfully, indicate that you're very familiar with the firm. If the inter viewer seems determined to provide you with background information despite your hints, and then listen attentively. If you can manage to initiate a brief, appropriate discussion of the company or industry at this point, that's great. It will help you to build rapport, underscore your interest, and increase your impact.

Soon the interviewer will begin to ask you questions. This period of the interview may be structured or unstructured, or somewhere in between. In a structured interview, the inter viewer asks a prescribed set of questions, seeking relatively brief answers. In the unstructured interview, the interviewer asks more open-ended questions to prod you into giving longer responses and revealing as much as possible about yourself, your background, and your aspirations. Some inter viewers will mix both styles, typically beginning with more objective questions and asking more open-ended questions as the interview progresses.

Try to determine as quickly as possible which direction the interviewer is going, and respond to the questions accordingly.

As you answer the questions, watch for signals from the employer as to whether your responses are too short or too long. For example, if the employer is nodding or looking away, wrap up your answer as quickly as possible. Following the style the interviewer establishes will make the interview easier and more comfortable and will help you make a more favourable impression.

Once you begin to feel more confident about interviewing, you may wish to think strategically about each interview. One effective tactic is to adjust your speed of speech to match that of the interviewer. People tend to talk at the speed at which they like to be spoken to. If you can adjust your speech rate to that of the recruiter without sounding unnatural, the recruiter will probably feel more comfortable (after all, interviewing others isn't much fun, either) and have a more favourable impression of you.

Another strategy is to adapt your answers to match the type of company for which you're interviewing. For example, if you're interviewing for a job at a large product-marketing company that emphasizes group decision making and spends much of its energy focused on battles for market share with its competitors, you might want to talk about how much you enjoy team sports—especially being part of a team and competing to win.

Concentrate on the themes you've developed in chapter 1 and be alert for opportunities to mention them. If applicable, draw parallels between your experience and the demands of the position as described by the interviewer. Talk about your past experience, emphasizing results and achievements and not merely recounting activities. If you listen carefully (listening is a crucial part of the interviewing process), the interviewer might very well give you an idea of the skills needed for the position. Don't exaggerate. Be on the level about your abilities.

Try not to be negative about anything during the inter view—especially about any past employer or previous job. Be cheerful. Everyone likes to work with someone who seems to be happy.

Don't let a tough question throw you off base. If you don't know the answer to a question, say so simply—don't apologize. Just smile. Nobody can answer every question—particularly some of the questions that are asked in job interviews.

Try not to cover too much ground during the first interview. This interview, in which many candidates are screened out, is often the toughest. If you're interviewing for a very competitive position, you'll have to make an impression that will last. Focus on a few of your greatest strengths that are relevant to the position. Develop these points carefully; state them again in different words, then try to summarize them briefly at the end of the interview.

Above all else, keep the conversations flowing. Don't talk too much or too little; watch the recruiter for signals. A job interview is a conversation between two people who are hoping to discover they have a common interest. Move around if you have to so that you don't appear stiff, but be careful not to fidget. Try to appear relaxed, enthusiastic, and determined—all at the same time!

The First Interview

As mentioned earlier, the first interview is often a screening interview conducted by a human-resources-department representative or an employment interviewer. The types of questions are general in nature—rarely specific to the technical aspects of the job. This is why it's important that you've developed themes related to the most relevant aspects of your own experiences and achievements. (See chapter 1 for more information on this strategy.)

The primary purpose of the first interview is to determine qualities like motivation, industry or functional skills, work ethic, communication skills, and critical-thinking skills. You should communicate genuine interest in the job, the industry, and the city or region of the country if relocation is part of the package. You need to demonstrate compatibility with the company culture and show that you can sell that compatibility in subsequent interviews if the recruiter moves you to the next round in the process. Recruiters are always concerned about weeding out any candidate who might embarrass them in a second interview; they must believe that they really got to know you and that you won't present any surprises in subsequent interviews. After all, their reputation and judgment are on the line if they recommend you for a second interview.

Strategies for Later Interviews

When filling professional career positions, few companies will make a job offer after only one interview. Usually, the purpose of the first interview is to narrow the field of applicants to a small number of very promising candidates. During the first meeting, then, the ideal strategy is to stand out from a large field of competitors in a positive way. The best way to do this is to emphasize subtly one or two of your key strengths as much as possible throughout the interview.

During later interviews, the competition for the position will drop off, and employers will tend to look not for strengths but for weaknesses. At this point, you should focus on presenting yourself as a well-balanced choice for the position.

Listen carefully to the interviewer's questions so you can determine his or her underlying concerns and try to dispel them. On the other hand, if later interviews are primarily with people who are in a position to veto your hiring, but not to push it forward, you should focus primarily on building rapport as opposed to reiterating and developing your key strengths.

Another way in which second interviews differ from first interviews is that the questions become much more specific and technical. The company must now test the depth of your knowledge of the field, including how well you're able to apply your education and past work experience to the job at hand. At this stage, the interviewer isn't a recruiter; you may have one or more interviewers, each of whom has a job related to the one you're applying for. Typically these interviewers will represent your potential boss, professional peer group, or executives who oversee the work group.

The second round of interviews can last one to two days, during which you might meet with as few as several people or as many as fifteen or more over the course of the visit.

These interviews typically last longer than initial interviews. For many executive positions, you may also have meetings around breakfast, lunch, or dinner. In all cases, remember you're still in an interview. You may be having a dinner conversation about a recent topic of concern to the industry as a whole—be ready with opinions, and be equally ready to listen and to ask good questions. You may be asked to demonstrate how you'd go about performing some aspect of the job; be ready in case you're presented with a tough problem and asked to tackle it as though you'd already started your first day on the job. Use what you said in the screening interview as an outline (it's gotten you this far!) but be prepared to build on this outline in meaningful ways with more developed details, examples, and ideas.

Usually you can count on attending at least two inter views for most professional positions, or three for high level positions, though some firms, such as some professional partnerships, are famous for conducting a minimum of six interviews for all professional positions. Though you should be more relaxed as you return for subsequent inter views, the pressure will still be on. The more prepared you are, the better.

Turning the Tables

Often the interviewer will pause toward the end and ask if you have any questions. Particularly in a structured interview, this might be the one chance to communicate your knowledge of, and interest in, the firm. Have a list prepared of specific questions that are of real interest to you. Let your questions subtly show your research and your knowledge of the firm's activities. It's wise to memorize an extensive list of questions, as several of them may be answered during the interview.

When asking the interviewer your questions, follow these guidelines:

- Don't let this opportunity turn into an interrogation. Don't bring your list of questions to the interview.
- Ask questions that you're fairly certain the interviewer can answer. (Remember how you feel when you can't answer a question during an interview.)
- If you're unable to determine the salary range before hand, don't ask about it during the first interview. You can always ask about it later.
- Don't ask about fringe benefits until you've been offered a position. (Then be sure to get all the details.) You should be able to determine the company's policy on benefits relatively easily before the interview.
- If it looks as though your skills and background don't match the position your interviewer was hoping to fill, ask if there's another division or subsidiary that perhaps could profit from your talents.

What questions should you ask? Here are some examples:

Q. "What position or positions does this job typically lead to?"

Q. 'Assuming I was hired and performed well for a number of years, what additional opportunities might this job lead to?"

These questions imply that you're an achievement-oriented individual looking for a company in which you can build a long-term career.

Q. "I've noticed in the trade press that your firm has a terrific reputation in marketing.

What are the major insights into the marketing process that I might gain from this position?"

Q. "I understand that your company is the market leader in industrial drill bits in North America. I'm curious to know how much of the product line is sold overseas—and whether there are many career opportunities in marketing abroad."

These questions imply that you're very interested in a long-term career in the industry and that you might lean toward pursuing a career with this firm because of its solid reputation. Your well-timed and appropriate questions are sure to impress even the toughest interviewer.

Q. "What skills are considered most useful for success in the job I'm applying for?"

This question implies that you really care about your success at your first job, and provides important information you can use to your advantage in the future.

Q. "I'd really like to work for your firm. I think it's a great company and I'm confident I could do this job well. What's the next step of the selection process?"

More than a question, this is a powerful statement that will quickly set you apart from other job hunters. However, you should make such a statement only if you mean it. If you're offered the position but then say you need two weeks to think it over, you'll lose your credibility. However, even after responding in this manner, it's reasonable to ask for one or two days to give an offer some thought.

Be sure to save your questions about salary, benefits, and related issues for later, after you receive an offer. You'll still be free to negotiate—or to decline the position—at that point

Also, avoid asking questions that will be difficult or awkward for the recruiter to answer. For example, this is not an appropriate time to ask, "Does your company use recycled paper for all its advertising brochures?"

A Final Note

Interviewing is like almost everything else—the more you do it, the better you become. Don't expect to give a perfect performance—especially in your first few interviews. Even experienced professionals who haven't interviewed in a while are bound to be rusty.

And if you have a terrible interview, don't let it shake your confidence! Remember that everyone has a bad interview experience sooner or later. Learn from it, work on your performance, and keep looking for other opportunities.

CHAPTER 6

The Essential Interview Questions

Okay, now you're ready to start practicing your interview questions. The following two hundred are among the most commonly asked questions in interviews today. If you can manage to get a good handle on these, you'll breeze through your interviews and really stand out from the crowd. Remember, employers are often interviewing many people for a single position, so you need to prepare answers that will get you noticed as a winner.

Chances are that a vast majority of the questions you'll be asked on a typical job interview appear in the next two chapters. But you may be asked a variation on one of our questions with different wording. Just remember as you work your way through the next sections that you're not trying to memorize the answers verbatim. Instead you are trying to respond to interview questions in a way that will convey that you're someone the employer would want to hire. In other words, project yourself as someone who's likely to stay with the company for a number of years, whose achievement oriented, who'll fit in well with the other employees, and who's likable.

Of course, you should also try to present yourself as someone who's capable of performing extremely well in the position.

You should avoid giving generic answers like "I'm a people person" or "I have excellent written and oral communication skills." Your response should always be specific (with supporting examples), and it should relate specifically to the job, the industry, or other personal factors to help your answer (and you!) stand out. Particularly in screening interviews, where generic questions are often asked, recruiters are looking to eliminate the average respondent. You can't afford a predictable, nondescript response. You must turn a common question into a memorable answer.

Go through the practice interview questions in the next two chapters. At first you may wish to read the sample responses and the accompanying discussion. Later, as you begin to feel more comfortable with the questions, try answering them without any help, as you would during a real interview.

1. Management Style and Interpersonal Skills

Q. Tell me about an effective manager, supervisor, or other person in a leading role you've known.

A. The best professor I ever had always reviewed the most important points from our last class before he moved on to new material. He also watched our faces carefully and repeated information whenever he saw a blank stare. Sometimes he would just ask for feedback by saying, "What are you having difficulty with?" He never assumed too much or made us feel dumb for not grasping a concept quickly.

Talk about a supervisor's management style and inter personal skills. Focus on the positive—how the person worked rather than what type of work he or she did. How was the person able to accomplish so much and get your support?

Q. What type of management style do you think is effective?

A. I've always learned well from people who act as coaches rather than experts. When someone comes to me with a problem, I try to act as if I'm reasoning through the problem with the person, learning as I go.

I never just give an answer. I want employees to develop confidence in creating answers for themselves.

This is similar to the question "Tell me about an effective manager or supervisor you've known." Give a personal or popular example of a leader you believe is effective. Why is this person able to accomplish so much? Talk about your management style and interpersonal skills with peer groups and leaders, and describe how you've incorporated habits from leaders you admire.

Q. Describe your personal management style.

A. I repeat what someone has told me, but I reorganize the information in a way that helps them see the problem or answer themselves. Sometimes I just ask questions until they see a clear solution. I learned this from watching a friend who's a successful trial lawyer.

Talk about your management style and interpersonal skills with peer groups and leaders, and describe how you've incorporated a habit from a leader you admire.

Q. What type of people do you work with most effectively?

A. I tend to work well with people who are confident and straight forward. It's more difficult for me to be around timid people, because I move quickly and am decisive.

Focus on the positive here. What type of boss, employee, and colleague would you be? Keep in mind that the inter viewer wants to find out how well you would fit in with the other personalities in the company—not how well the other personalities in the company would suit you.

Q. What things impress you in colleagues?

A. I admire and work best with people who are of good character and have integrity. I also think confidence and enthusiasm is positive in any business environment.

The recruiter will want to see how developed your interpersonal skills are. More than likely, you'll be interacting not only with your own department, but with other people in the company, and possibly colleagues. Show the recruiter that you will shine in this area.

Q. What are some of the things your supervisor did that you disliked?

A. The only thing I really don't like is to get feedback in front of others. I want to hear good or bad feedback in private, so that I have time to think and react to the issue without other distractions. I believe that's the fair way to improve learning or to change future behaviour.

Try to describe a positive learning experience from a difficult situation, avoiding personal criticism of an ex-boss or manager, if possible.

Q. How do you organize and plan for major projects?

A. I love to brainstorm a best, worst, and most likely scenario. Then I set a timetable that's realistic. What I usually find is that some combination of my best and worst cases evolves; I can adjust my schedule easily as these things unfold because I've already visualized what could happen and how I'd react.

Give the interviewer a good idea of your general approach to mastering complex tasks. You may wish to include here how you decide on time frames, set deadlines, determine priorities, delegate tasks, and decide what to do for yourself.

Q. Describe a time when you've worked under intense pressure.

A. I had to complete an end-of-quarter report once while I was on the road for two consecutive weeks. The amount of telephoning back and forth was incredible, because I couldn't bring my office files with me.

Luckily I had a great secretary and a logical filing system, so we located everything we needed.

A good idea when answering a question like this is to concentrate on your time-management skills. Give a specific example, with enough detail to communicate both the intensity of the situation and the ease with which you handled it.

Q. How do you manage your time on a typical day?

A. I've always given priority to work with established clients, because they offer a better risk/return value.

The last thing I do is general correspondence, especially internal correspondence, which I take care of at the end of the day or week.

Here the interviewer wants evidence that the candidate can juggle priorities as necessary based on the work team, departmental adjustments, and nature of the tasks. He or she will also want to be sure that you don't give priority to fun work and avoid dull, necessary routines that are important in the long run.

Q. Describe a time when you acted on someone's suggestion.

A. I changed my open office hours because several of my employees found it difficult to visit me except in the early mornings.

Be specific here in demonstrating your flexibility and your interpersonal skills. Do people feel comfortable offering you suggestions? Do they believe you'll listen fairly and objectively? When you do take their advice, do you give credit where credit is due? Reassure the interviewer that your approach to management is reasonable and fair, and that you respect other people's good ideas.

Q. Tell me about a time when you had to defend an idea to your boss.

A. Once I had to convince my boss to change PR firms. I really believed that our interests on the West Coast weren't being met by our Chicago-based firm. I was able to convince him after showing him the demographic shift in our customer base.

This is the flip side of "Describe a time when you acted on someone's suggestion." Can you give advice constructively and get someone to understand your side? Give a specific example.

Q. What aspect of your management style would you like to change?

A. I've been working on holding back the urge to tell people the answers when they ask for advice. I think it's more important to teach people how to solve their own problems. I've gotten better at coaching and presenting questions and feedback without telling people what to do.

Talk about one aspect of your management style that you're working to improve. Tell the interviewer the steps you're taking and give evidence that you're making progress.

Q. Have you ever felt defensive around your boss or peers?

A. I had to explain once why I thought a black-and white brochure was more suitable for the content of an insurance-product brochure. No one in my office liked the idea initially, because we were all used to colour brochures, and everybody felt that black and white looked cheap. Eventually I convinced them that a more subtle approach would work better to present information about a difficult topic—death benefits.

Pick a specific example of a time when you had to defend an idea. Avoid any discussion of personality clashes, feelings of resentment, or heated exchanges. How did you get others to see your view of things? What was the outcome? Be sure to end on a positive note.

Q. Tell me about a learning experience that affected your management style.

A. Early in my job at the bank, I wrote a letter to an EVP but failed to make copies for the two AVPs who worked for him. One of them was impacted by the content of the memo and concluded that I'd circumvented him on purpose. I've really been careful about chain of command ever since.

Use a variation of your answer to the question "Tell me about your least-favourite manager or supervisor," in which you describe an experience, either positive or negative, that taught you a lesson about effective management. Or describe the tactics of a manager who got you to perform more than you thought was possible. How did he or she motivate you?

Q. Have you patterned your management style after someone in particular?

A. I've emulated my first boss in many ways. I keep a file for each member of my staff on my desk. They can throw notes, ideas, work they want me to review or anything else in there, and I do the same with material I have for them. It's an extra form of communication whenever one of us gets an idea. Then, when we sit down to talk, the issues we need to cover are in one place, at our fingertips.

Your answer should describe someone you've known personally—a boss who motivated you in a positive way to achieve beyond your own goals. Be specific about how he or she accomplished this.

Q. Describe a leader you admire.

A. I've always admired the president of my company. He's visible, he doesn't want a special parking place or table in the cafeteria, and he gives you the feeling that he's just another member of the team.

Give personal or popular examples of leaders you believe are effective. Why do you believe those people are able to accomplish so much? What tricks have you learned from the leaders you admire?

Q. What personal characteristics add to your effectiveness?

A. I always stay in touch with my network. I see an article that might be of interest to someone I know, I clip it and send it to that person. Then, when I need help and make a phone call to that person, the phone call gets returned promptly.

Talk about what makes your personal style unique and effective. For example, how are you able to get cooperation from others? What specific skills and traits help you get results, and why?

2. Problem-Solving Ability

Q. How have your technical skills been an asset?

A. Although I never planned on a career as a writer or publisher, much of my job in marketing has depended on good writing and creative layout skills. My part-time college job with a newspaper taught me a lot about desktop publishing, how to position something on a page effectively, and how to write short sentences with maximum impact. In all of my marketing jobs, I've been able to explain my goals clearly a too graphic designer, which has helped me avoid costly design revisions.

Describe how you've used technical skills to solve a problem. Tell a specific story. Demonstrate how these same skills have been useful in other situations or in most of the jobs you've held. If you're hired, what situations will you handle particularly well?

Q. Describe a situation in which you've applied technical skills to solve a problem.

A. One of our components kept arriving at distribution points with stress cracks. My materials science background helped me to diagnose the problem as one of storage temperature during shipping. Although our equipment was safely stored at both end points, it had been sitting in un-air-conditioned cargo space for up to thirty hours before reaching its destination. We're now using a different shipping company, and we've improved our labelling on large shipments to reflect the user's warning about temperature extremes.

Quickly define the problem for the interviewer, and then focus on how your skills enabled you to tackle it. What actions did you take, and what was the outcome?

Q. How do your technical skills, combined with other skills, add to your effectiveness on the job?

A. My strong economic background, along with my computer-sales experience, provides a balanced set of skills to perform financial research on the computer Industry. Most of my contacts and hobbies are also related to high tech, so I offer a natural curiosity that helps me stay abreast of changes in the industry.

This question gives you a chance to sell the package deal—why is the unique combination of your skills effective? Give one or two specific examples of projects you're frequently asked to handle.

Q. Describe how you've used a problem-solving process.

A. We once had several customers who'd arranged numerous free hotels stays around the country using our 100 percent satisfaction guarantee. I suggested leading a PC task force to set up a warning system that flags any guest name corresponding to a previous reported complaint or free service. Now when a guest checks in and we type in a name, we know immediately that the person has had an unpleasant experience at one of our hotels. We proactively approach the guest, acknowledge we're aware of the problem, and offer our commitment to do everything possible to provide them with impeccable service. This practice warns the potentially fraudulent guest; at the same time, it warns our staff to be especially careful with any guest who's giving our hotel a second chance. Our satisfaction rate has improved, and fraudulent cases have decreased.

Describe for the interviewer, step by step, how a problem solving process you initiated came to a successful conclusion.

What measures or benchmarks did you use to control or man age the process? What were the results?

Q. How do you usually go about solving a problem?

Al When I need to solve a problem, I generally start by writing down as many ideas as I can think of about possible causes. Next I look for relationships among causes so I can group together symptoms of bigger problems. Usually, after I study these groups of problems, the real cause becomes readily apparent

The interviewer will want to hear the logic you use to solve problems as well as the outcomes you're able to achieve. Are you decisive? How do you narrow the options and make decisions? What do people say about your reasoning skills? What examples would they cite of your effective decision making?

Q. How do you measure the success of your work?

A. I measure reactions of customers. When my customers call me with a referral, I know they're happy. And I have to say that repeat business to me is more satisfying than winning a new account People have a tendency to try a new company because of that company's reputation or product, but they come back because of the relationship they've learned to trust.

What results or evidence do you need to evaluate the success of your work? What type of feedback or reward system is important to you? The reviewer will want to establish that these needs can be satisfied in the job.

Q. How practical or pragmatic are you?

A. I can usually pick up on an underlying problem, even if it's not too obvious. I recall an investment banker who visited our real-estate-finance class and asked us might cause the Tokyo investment community a problem in attracting local investment dollars. A number of finance M.B. A.'s in the class started trying to think of some complicated set of reckons. I decided it would have to do with getting out of a bad market quickly, and that a non liquid investment would create problems. I said investors would be unsettled if the primary investment is local real estate and inflation has caused the paper value to exaggerate the real street value. As it ended up, that was the answer he wanted.

Give the interviewer an example of some practical or sensible approach you've used to solve a problem. When was a simple solution the best solution? Had others overlooked the obvious? In this example, you'll want to show off your common sense skills rather than your academic skills.

Q. How do you balance your reliance on facts with your reliance on intuition?

A. Facts are important but often neglect point-in-time influences, especially with market research. One survey that I was uncomfortable with involved pricing data that was collected just after a major presidential election. The timing caused me to doubt that consumers would really spend as much as the survey indicated they would for new cars. So we ended up holding on to the last quarter's pricing structure. We sold more cars while, as interest rates climbed, some of our competitors had expensive inventory carry over.

Describe a specific time when your intuition helped you solve a problem that might have been handled badly if you'd followed the facts or standard procedure. Demonstrate an ability to "think outside of the box."

Q. What was your greatest problem in your last job?

A. I had to get long time employees with few or no computer skills to embrace a new e-mail system. I started by explaining the need for less paper in everyone's job. Then I decided to create a temporary e-mail account with one daily riddle on the system; everyone who responded correctly got their name put in a weekly drawing. Each week for one month a person from the drawing got dinner for four at a nice local restaurant. This approach went over well as a device to get people to use the system.

The interviewer wants to hear about a problem area the candidate improved in his or her last job. If you're asked this question, don't complain without showing solutions.

Demonstrate an ability to offer solutions, not merely to point out problems.

Q. Tell me about a problem that you failed to anticipate.

A. My boss asked me to solve an ongoing scheduling problem. I failed to realize that the person who had lived with the problem would see me as an antagonist

By the time I realized it, I'd already done some of the ground work. If I'd started by asking for the person's opinion, I would have been able to get him on my side early on.

This question forces you to be humble but gives you an opportunity to relate an incident from which you learned an important lesson. What warning signs should you have seen?

How has your judgment improved as a result of this experience?

Q. Have you ever resolved a long-standing problem?

A. We used to batch our guests' personal faxes—sometimes as many as ten out going fax requests per hour—to put less strain on our administrative staff.

We had guests who weren't happy about that I arranged a lease deal on an outgoing fax machine for guest self-serve access. This freed up more time for staff, and they were able to maintain control of incoming faxes, protecting incoming information until they could locate the appropriate guest in person.

Tell the interviewer about a problem you championed within a work setting or other organization. How did you overcome or circumvent the obstacles? What were the results?

What motivated you to tackle the problem to begin with?

Q. Describe a time you found it necessary to make an unpopular decision.

A. I had to start a policy of no food in work areas, including private offices, because the production workers were unhappy with the inequity. For safety reasons workers couldn't have food anywhere near expensive equipment. Now it's forgotten, but at the time a number of supervisors were angry at me. I thought the matter was important and that the solution was consistent with other new policies, like doing away with assigned parking spaces for high level employees. So far we've been progressive enough to keep unions out of our company.

Sometimes an important long-term result is achieved only with short-term sacrifices. This question measures the candidate's ability to make important value judgments with long term results. Be sure to give a specific example if you're asked a question like this.

Q. Tell me about the most difficult problem you've ever dealt with.

A. I was promoted to manage a new department A co-worker in that group resented me from the beginning. I soon learned that her best friend had been turned down for the position. I actually confronted her about it; I explained that I had once put a friendship to the test because I'd worked too closely with someone and we found that we spent our leisure time talking about work. A few weeks after our talk, she admitted that she'd never thought about the potential results of working too closely with a personal friend. Our working relationship wets fine after that.

Discuss the problem here briefly, and then focus on what actions you took and what results you obtained. Be candid— why was this problem personally hard for you? How did you remain objective and professional?

Q. Describe a time when a problem wasn't resolved to your satisfaction.

A. I thought once that we'd let a customer down by not responding quickly enough to resolve a problem; our production capacity wasn't sufficient to deliver the customer's complete order during the holiday season.

That customer ended up asking for a discount, and I thought we should have offered the discount first, without waiting to be asked. The sense of goodwill would have been stronger.

This question focuses on the candidate's standards of quality. Describe a situation in which you foresaw long-term complications from a problem that was poorly handled. Did you do anything to try to resolve the issue?

Q. Tell me about a time when there was no rule or precedent to help you attack a problem.

A. I was the first employee in a newly created position. I spent the first week developing an understanding of the history that had led to creation of the position. Only then did a method for setting priorities on the job become clear.

Can you operate without structure? Describe your problem-solving process, especially the steps you took and measures you established in a particularly trying situation.

Demonstrate confidence and the willingness to take on new challenges.

Q. When do you have difficulty making choices?

A. I'm not particularly good at interpreting survey data. I've really worked to get to know our research staff and librarians. I rely on them and am careful to thank them formally in front of my vice president.

We're definitely a team, and I'm careful not to take credit for our industry reports, which we publish for the Pacific region of our firm.

Be honest. What situations are difficult for you to resolve?

What people, or other resources, do you gather in these instances to help you make decisions?

Q. Describe an opportunity in which you felt the risks far outweighed the rewards.

A. A tone point we had an opportunity to purchase conveyor equipment at thirty cents on the dollar from a company that had dissolved. Although we anticipated an overhaul of our distribution facility five years down the road, I felt it was too far into the future to spend money only to have idle capacity for a five-year period. If market conditions had shown more promise for new sales in the initial two-year period, I would have gone ahead with it.

The interviewer wants to see that the candidate has an interest in taking reasonable risks without inclining toward foolishness. Demonstrate with an example your logic for deciding against some plan. How was the outcome preferable to what might have happened?

3. Accomplishments

Q. Tell me about a major accomplishment.

A. I'm really proud of the business I obtained with XYZ Wholesale Club. I believe that these types of companies will continue to thrive in the next few years.

Offer proof of your accomplishments using real examples.

Don't give long descriptions of situations. Focus your answer on the actions you took and the positive results you obtained.

The interviewer will want to know what you can contribute to the company.

Q. Talk about a contribution you've made to a team.

A. I helped my last team put together more cohesive presentations for a client I think our practice and preparation made a statement about how committed we would be to the details of the system installation. In the end, we landed the account.

Tell the interviewer about your initiative within a team. Offer proof, using specific examples, that you delivered more than the team expected and that the team would compliment your contributions to the group's efforts. What special role did you play?

Q. Talk about a special contribution you've made to an employer.

A: In my last job Iran the United Way campaign for three consecutive years. I believe it's an important cause, and I know it's difficult for the company to find volunteers, so I stepped in.

Let the interviewer know that you deliver more than your employer expects. If you were hired, what situations would you handle especially well? What unique contributions can you make to the organization? How would you go the extra mile?

Q. Tell me about an organization outside of work that's benefited from your participation.

A. I've been involved in Junior Achievement. I was an economics undergrad, and I liked seeing the high school kids get excited about what they read in the paper and about how economics affects their lives.

Discuss in some detail your initiative with something you volunteered for—such as working for a charitable organization. In other words, what things are important motivators for you? Could your employer benefit from these interests in some way? What kind of corporate citizen are you?

Q. Give me an example of a time you delivered more than was expected.

A. In my last job my boss asked me to take over all the uncollected accounts. I wets able to recover 20 percent more than his goal. I convinced people that I was willing to work out an affordable schedule based on their needs, and I did this by asking about their problems. Once they vented, they would usually listen to me.

Give an example of a time when you truly excelled at a given task. Chances are you're likely to repeat similar results in your new position. In other words, give the interviewer an indication of the situations you might handle especially well if you were hired.

Q. What accomplishment is your greatest source of pride?

A. I'm proud of how we turned a profit at our hospital in the first year under private management. Now that goal's been accomplished, and I'm ready to do the same for another hospital; that's why consulting within the industry appeals to me so much.

Your answer will hint at the kinds of projects you'd like to do in the future. Focus on goals related specifically to the job you're applying for. The interviewer will want to know how your past initiative and accomplishments can translate to success for his or her company.

Q. If I hired you today, what would you accomplish first?

A. I could help you increase your business within the OEM market. As an OEM contractor for four years, I understand how to structure deals that will be profitable.

Give the interviewer clear, tangible evidence that the company will benefit immediately upon hiring you. Focus your answer on the action you would take, and make sure your goals are realistic. Can you demonstrate specific knowledge about the company and industry and how it relates to the role of your department and job?

Q. What accomplishment was the most difficult for you to achieve?

A. I found it intimidating to work with the marketing research staff when I started my job, mostly because I hadn't done well in statistics or market research during college. What I decided to do was enroll in an executive seminar on market research, which really boosted my confidence. Now I don't feel at a disadvantage when I meet with the research group, and I know what questions to ask to get information that's meaningful to me.

Describe something you've accomplished despite obstacles, lack of training, or inadequate experience. This question allows you to talk about overcoming a weakness.

Q. Tell me about a time you saved money for an employer or an organization.

A. I was able to eliminate a middleman we'd worked with for years in getting our employee magazine printed. We planned the issues, collected research, wrote the articles, did most of the editing, and then handed the information to him, which he took to a designer and printer. After I managed this process twice, I decided to do the coordinating work myself.

The additional time it cost me was eight hours, but we saved a 10 percent mark up, and even better, the issues now get completed faster and with greater accuracy.

Be specific and quantify your results when answering your question, but don't give long descriptions of situations. Offer proof using a clear, convincing example.

Q. What's your greatest achievement to date?

A. I'm proud of the fact that I graduated on time with a solid GPA while I played varsity basket ball for four years. A lot of the women on my team either took a reduced course load or let their grades suffer. I believe the reason I got through it all was sheer determination; I never even let myself visualize anything but finishing on time and with good grades.

So I firmly believe, as a professional counsellor, in the importance of a positive outlook.

Be sure that the achievement you describe here is relevant to the job you're interviewing for. Also, be careful that your answer doesn't sound as if the best is behind you. Mention something great that you've achieved, but clearly communicate your belief that the best is yet to come.

Q. Tell me about a person or group you had to work with to achieve something important.

A. My law-school class really worked hard to improve the image of our school with employers. We put together our own promotional book, which we sent to Law firms and alumni. The book presented a mock courtroom case in which other law schools filed a class-action suit arguing that the quality of the student body and teaching at our school had caused an erosion of interest in other law programs; they proved to the court that both teaching and student statistics clearly had led to positive placements for our graduates, which in turn killed the chances for students from other programs. The format of our brochure was so unusual that it got the attention of the major press, which served our purpose nicely.

Give an example that demonstrates your use of teamwork to produce a better result than you could have achieved by yourself. Acknowledge your contributions and those of your team members.

Q. Tell me about something you accomplished that required discipline.

A. J had to work two jobs to put myself through graduate school. I interned at the newspaper while I studied journalism during the week. Then on weekends, I sold real estate. Juggling those three schedules was a challenge, but I did it because it was important to me to graduate without school loans.

This is your opportunity to discuss a skill you worked to develop, or a time when the quantity of your work required solid time-management skills. How did you remain focused?

Q. What situations do your colleagues rely on you to handle?

A. People often rely on me to handle client confrontations. I'm known as a person who never loses my temper in front of customers.

This question provides a good opportunity for the candidate to showcase his or her dependability, strength of character, and professionalism. The interviewer will be impressed if you can also demonstrate that you work well with others and clearly enjoy your colleagues' respect.

Q. Tell me about a need you fulfilled within a group or a committee.

A. I worked on the committee to review our company's policy on sick leave. One of our employees was abusing the system in order to gain vacation time. I served as the objective member of the group, having used virtually no sick leave in five years of employment. I ended up presenting an idea that the company's now considering, which is to allow up to one week of sick time to be voluntarily allocated to extra family-leave time.

Tell the interviewer about your initiative in group projects.

In teams, what roles do you usually play?

Q. Tell me how you've supported and helped attain a corporate goal.

A. J helped meet our goal of value to stockholders by holding a fire sale of goods to cleanout our warehouse.

The public was invited, with a preview for customers, suppliers, vendors, and stockholders. Attendees bought new but visually imperfect electronics components at 70 percent reductions. We cleared twenty thousand Dollars from sales of equipment we'd written off.

Here the interviewer asks for evidence that the candidate completes projects with the corporation's goals in mind. What other groups, departments, or customers benefited from a similar effort on your part? Give specific examples, not generalizations. Focus on how you've enriched your job by expanding the benefits of your action beyond your own group or department.

Q. Tell me about a quantifiable outcome of one of your efforts.

A. I reorganised inventory planning and was able to automate the inventory-reorder function, which used to be a forty-hour process and now takes only three hours.

Describe a specific accomplishment, the outcome of which produced a clear benefit. Offer proof, using real examples, that you deliver more than what's expected. Did you exceed your expected outcome? How?

Q. Describe an ongoing problem you were able to overcome.

A. We had three groups with different home grown schedules, even though each group relied on the others' work and timing. I got us all connected via a computer network and held a training session to brain storm our communications plan. We now talk regularly via e-mail and a network scheduler, and we all have the information we need.

This question is similar to "Tell me about a time you tack led an unpopular assignment." Focus on how you achieved good results through the use of a creative technique or through greater diligence than others had previously devoted to the project.

Q. Tell me about a project you completed ahead of schedule.

A. I was in charge of a new product rollout. In general we completed each phase without a major setback—which was partially luck—but I also systematically called two days ahead of every deadline to check the status with all groups involved. I believe that made the difference. The launch took place two weeks ahead of plan—a significant period of time in our industry, where shelf life for products is generally less than one year.

Focus here on how you set goals and schedules, measured results, and championed the outcome of a project. This question is aimed at your diligence in accomplishing tasks and, assuming the project required group effort, at your leadership skills.

4. Career Aspirations

Q. Where do you hope that your career will have progressed to in the next few years?

A. Over the next few years I'd like to have progressed to the point where I have bottom-line budget responsibility, and I'm also in charge of a production unit where I have labour-relations, quality-control, design, and manufacturing responsibilities. I believe this job will go a long way to helping me meet my career goals.

Avoid the temptation to suggest job titles; this makes you seem unbending and unrealistic, since you don't know or control the system of promotion. Likewise, you don't know how long it might have taken your interviewer to reach certain levels, and you wouldn't want to insult. Describe new experiences or responsibilities you'd like to add that build on the job you're applying for.

Q. What are your long-term career plans?

A. My long-term career goals are to become known as an industry expert and to have earned a respectable management position with responsibility for a major piece of the business. I'd like to think I'll have experience in many parts of the business over time.

It's reasonable to see ahead about five years but probably no more, given the changing nature of businesses. Especially in high-tech fields, which change dramatically in a short time, it's impossible to project accurately how you might fit into a specific job. Therefore, focus on types of experiences you hope to gain over time.

Q. Since this will be your first job, how do you know you'll like the career path?

A. Although it's true that I've never worked a job in your industry, I've talked to many friends and alums at my school that've been successful in your company. I always ask them the questions, "What's the most frustrating thing about your job?" and "What's the most rewarding thing about your job?" From the information I've gained, I'm confident that I'll be able to adapt quickly to your culture and will find the next few years rewarding, based on my goals and values.

This can be a difficult question to answer convincingly, unless you've done a little bit of preparation. Discuss, for example, an internship or a conversation that's allowed you to assess the culture of the organization or to preview the work involved. Describe other people in the profession who have been mentors or who have taught you about the field.

Also, point out why you're interested, how you learned more about the industry, and how you stay current with industry trends.

Q. Why is this job right for you at this time in your career?

A. This job would build on my extensive technical background both as a navy communications officer and in the two software companies where I've worked.

I believe I'm now ready to assume broader responsibilities as a project manager. I've demonstrated my ability to handle the responsibility for both a diverse team of programmers and engineers and for major capital budgets.

Describe the experiences you want to pursue that build on your current skills and interests. Be as specific as you can, based on what you know about the current or future direction of the position and the department. Demonstrate why this position fits with your personal career goals. How can you create job growth for yourself?

Q. What are your aspirations beyond this job?

A. Beyond this job as marketing assistant, I see myself moving up through marketing analysis into brand management and eventually running a category. I'm aware that there are several skills I need to develop in the interval, and I believe with your continuing education program and my own motivation for self improvement,

I'll have those skills when the opportunities arise for greater responsibility. That's why I'm determined to learn from the ground up, starting as a marketing assistant.

Again, don't fall into the trap of specifying job titles. Stick to a natural progression you see as plausible. How should this job grow for the good of the organization? Then turn your attention once again to the job at hand. If you seem too interested in what lies beyond this job, the interviewer will fear that you won't stick around for long.

Q. What new challenges would you enjoy?

A. I've worked in the hospitality industry for over eight years and have progressively worked in larger, more prestigious hotels. I've learned the food-and-beverage side of the business and the hotel-management side, and now I believe I'm ready to be a convention- or conference-sales manager.

Describe the natural next step in your skill development based on what you've learned and enjoyed in your last job. What do you feel ready to tackle next? Be as specific as you can, considering what you know about the current or future direction of the position and department.

Q. If you could start all over again, what direction would your career take?

A. I've always enjoyed consumer sales as I've moved up in my career. Looking back, I wish I'd gotten a bit more experience in market research earlier in my career, because it's important to understand the types of quantitative models and technical-research techniques that are now important for a regional sales manager to know.

The interviewer will want to see if your career path is less than ideal for you. Be careful to show that your heart lies in this field, but offer some insights so that someone else following in your foot steps might quicken the learning curve, time frame, and so on.

Q. What achievements have eluded you?

Al I've achieved considerable success at the finance department of my company, a large corporation. I've worked in two different plants as the director of finance. I've worked in capital budgets at the corporate office and in the business-planning area.

Unfortunately, I've never had the opportunity to work in the treasury department. Based on my graduate finance education and my several years' finance experience, I'm now convinced that I'm ready to handle this responsibility and that it'll be the next step in my learning curve toward a top finance executive position.

Describe a responsibility you'd like but haven't yet earned.

What do you feel ready to tackle next? Explain why you haven't yet had the opportunity to assume such a responsibility, but take care not to sound passive. Describe some continuing efforts to reach your goals. Ask yourself, would your current employer agree that you're ready?

Q. How long do you think you'd continue to grow in this job?

A. My own personal measure of growth in a job is acquiring new skills, new knowledge, and new insights into the industry As long as I can measure this type of growth, I consider myself successful. I'm a believer in stretching a job by reaching out to learn more about other areas that are peripheral to the job I'm in.

This is a variation on the question "Where do you want to be in five years?" Be as specific as you can, considering what you know about the position. Don't mention a job title you'd want next, or the interviewer will wonder if you're already preoccupied with moving on.

Q. What career path interests you within the company?

A. I'd like to work toward becoming a senior project manager within your commercial real-estate firm. My background includes several areas within commercial real estate, including working in architectural design, working with governmental departments and agencies, working with banks in the finance area, and, finally, working in sales and leasing. I'd like to pull all this background together in the next few years and eventually have project-management responsibility.

Demonstrate your knowledge of the typical career path, if you're familiar with it. If not, turn this answer into a question: "What's the typical career path for someone with my skills?" Focus principally on businesses or divisions of the company that interest you, as well as skills and challenges you hope to master in the next few years.

Q. Compare this job to others you're pursuing.

A. I've narrowed my job search to only those large securities firms within the finance industry. The basic skills necessary with all of these firms are similar:

Strong quantitative and analytical abilities, the ability to make decisions quickly, and good interpersonal skills to react to a customer's needs

Some consistency or thread of commonality among your other prospects is important here. Your choices must reflect your career aspirations.

What common skills are clearly needed in all the jobs you're pursuing?

Q. Have you progressed in your career as you expected?

A. My six years with a major gas company have included solid experience in price analysis, capital budgets, and financial planning. I now believe I'm ready to take on departmental responsibility for the entire finance function within a finance company.

Review the positive learning experiences from your past jobs and the next steps you're ready to take as a result, but also be realistic in admitting the areas where you need more experience. Honesty—without demonstrating either pessimism or unrealistic expectations—is important here.

Q. Tell me about your salary expectations.

A. I've become a little frustrated in the past year because the downturn in our industry has caused limited promotional opportunities. Based upon salary information published by our national association, the market price for someone with my experience and educational background is in the broad range of thirty to forty thousand dollars per year. Although I'm not certain how your salaries compare to the national norms, my feeling is that my value would certainly be in the upper half of this national range. I hope you'll share with me some of your salary ranges relative to the national norms.

A well-prepared candidate can effectively turn this question around. Ask first for the company's salary range, and then answer in general terms based on your qualifications in relation to the job requirements.

Q. What do you reasonably expect to earn within five years?

Al My expectation for the next five years is that my contributions will be recognized and appropriately rewarded. I realize that salary levels are based on a number of factors, including the company's profitability and the general business cycle that affects our industry, but I expect to take on greater responsibility each year and to be appropriately compensated for my efforts and contributions.

Again, turn this question around and ask what's typical for the career path. Then consider, based on your skills and performance, the areas you'll excel in. Leave it to the interviewer to determine the appropriate time frames for promotions.

Don't speculate, or you'll risk sounding arrogant, unrealistic, or the opposite—too reserved or too tentative.

Q. Have you ever taken a position that didn't fit into your long-term plan?

A. Back in the late eighties, when Wall Street was booming, I was lured away with a high-paying offer in a firm that was trading commodities on the Asian market. Even though I had success in the job, I quickly realized that the work wasn't fulfilling or challenging enough to keep me happy. So, after two years, I jumped back into the corporate world as a controller for one of the metal plants of my corporation. I've since moved up in the finance area, and my long-term plans include staying in this industry and assuming greater responsibility in the area of financial planning and control.

The interviewer is trying to determine here how wisely the candidate can pick jobs to match his or her interests and aspirations. If you've been sidetracked by some job, you'll probably have to convince the recruiter that you're on the right track pursuing this position.

5. Personal Interests and Hobbies

Q. Other than work, tell me about an activity you've remained interested in over several years.

A. I've been involved in Cancer Society fundraising ever since my grandmother died from the disease. In the back of my mind I guess I'm hoping that the research and lead to findings in time to save the life of someone else in my family.

The interviewer is looking here for a history of commitment over time, and consistency of interests. Do you sustain your hobbies over a period of time, or do you have a different hobby every year? Are your interests compatible with the job you're applying for? Would they be of value in any way to the company?

Q. What do you do in your spare time?

A. I really enjoy getting outside—J often go camping and hiking. I've learned a lot about different fabrics that are good for various weather conditions. That's why I'm so interested in your textile operations.

The interviewer wants evidence that you're well rounded, not just one-dimensional. He or she is also looking for shared interests or common ground. You should always, in some way, relate your answer to the job description.

Q. Do you have a balanced lifestyle?

A. I make an effort to get out of the office at a reasonable hour twice a week. I go home and walk my dog. That's one of the most relaxing things I do, but it often helps me think of solutions for problems at work, even though I'm not consciously trying to solve those problems.

Do you have an outlet, a way to get a break from work, so that you show up each day refreshed and ready to perform at your highest level? Describe something specific that allows you to relax. Are your personal and career interests compatible in terms of their logic or thought processes

Q. What outside activities complement your work interests?

A. I've always enjoyed tennis. In many ways it's a game of strategy and pacing. When something isn't working in the first set, you have to change your strategy for the second set. You also have to pace your energy in case you go to a third set, and constantly watch and read your opponent's reactions. I'm a gutsy tennis player—go for the big points sometimes—but I'm careful with timing. That's the way I am at work, too.

The interviewer is interested to see if the candidate's personality is reflected in both work and outside activities. Your answer to this question will shed light on your personality and thus possibly on your compatibility with the job.

Q. Tell me about a time you were in a recreational setting and got an idea that helped in your work.

A. I was on vacation in Mexico and saw a woman with a homemade seesaw she was using to lift her laundry basket when she needed something out of it. It gave me an idea for a new type of scaffolding, which I designed when I got back to work. Now our brick masons have a rotating bench that keeps their materials at waist level, which reduces back fatigue.

The interviewer will want to know if you have the ability to synthesize information and apply what you see to your profession. Show that your work is something you're naturally inquisitive about, rather than something you have to do.

Are you able to "think outside of the box" to come up with fresh ideas? Be sure to give specific examples.

Q. How is your personality reflected in the kinds of activities you enjoy?

A. L love to cook and entertain. That's the salesman coming out in me. I love sharing experiences with people, and I'm very outgoing. I don't particularly enjoy being alone.

I always feel as if I should be doing something.

Describe how your natural skills and values are reflected in various things you do, from work to leisure. What are your comfortable patterns of operating? For example, a detailed, precise hobby reflects something different from a risk oriented, aggressive sport.

Q. What kinds of leisure activities help you perform your work better?

A. I enjoy sitting outside during lunch and talking with students. It gives me a chance to get fresh air, but it also helps the students get comfortable with me, so they're more likely to seek my help when they need it.

The recruiter will want to know that you have an outlet to relax. Just about any hobby or leisure activity will help you perform more efficiently at work, but if you can tie the activity directly to job performance, so much the better.

Q. What do you do to relax?

A. I have a great family. Weekends are like a vacation for me. When I'm at work, I focus on work, but when I'm home on weekends, work really is far from my mind.

One of the smartest things I did was to move twenty miles outside of town; even the drive home is relaxing.

An admission that work is far from your mind when you're relaxing is not necessarily a bad thing. This candidate attractively reveals additional information about his or her character and, at the same time, lets the interviewer know that there is plenty of psychic energy stored for the work day.

Q. If you found yourself getting burned out, what would you do to revitalize your energy?

A. I don't allow myself to get involved in a routine to the point that I get burned out. I've always been the type of person who asks for new assignments so that I stay motivated and interested.

Are you disciplined enough to avoid burnout? When you're not being productive, do you recognize it? What do you do to cope with stress?

Q. Our company believes that employees should give time back to the community. How do you feel about it?

A. I believe that, too. In my last job as manager I told each of my employees that they could spend one Friday afternoon a month at a charity of their choice on company time as long as they weren't all gone on the same Fridays. Ironically, productivity didn't decrease at all; they got more done in the morning—and I guess Friday afternoons weren't that productive to begin with. I've spent my afternoons with an adult reading program.

Describe a time you gave something to a community or organization as a volunteer. Do you go above and beyond what's expected of you? Do you use your skills productively?

Are you unselfish—a team player? Demonstrate how your personal interests make you productive even when you aren't being paid. What incentives other than a pay check inspire you?

Q. What community projects that can use your professional skills are particularly interesting to you?

A: As a marketing person, I've offered free advice to our local high school for its fund-raisers, as well as to a local real-estate office whose success could help my rural community's real-estate values.

This interviewer wants to know if the candidate will be a good corporate citizen. The question also gives the interviewer a sense of the job seeker's values. Try to focus your answer on productive applications of your work-related skills. Don't get sidetracked describing a cause that doesn't demonstrate job related skills. Avoid discussing any charity or organization that may be considered controversial.

Q. If you had unlimited leisure time, how would you spend that time?

A. I don't think I could ever be happy with lots of spare time. I'd probably travel, learn another language, and spend more time with my two charities. I'd also take more courses in accounting.

In answering this question, demonstrate that you'd use your time to increase your skills, or to give something back to the community or a good cause. When possible, choose an activity that's career- or job-oriented; for example, if you're in marketing, say you'd get involved with Junior Achievement and teach young people about careers in business. Your answer should reflect your energy and capacity for work, as well as your natural curiosity. Don't say something like "I don't know; I'd just like to relax."

Q. Describe how a sport or hobby taught you a lesson in teamwork or discipline.

A. My football coach from high school taught me always to watch out for the other guy. If you do, he'll cover you when you need him to. I've applied that principle in all my work groups, especially on the trading floor.

Tell about a time you had to use teamwork to get a desired result. Tell a specific story, and then explain how the same skill or lesson has been used in your work.

Q. When you aren't at work, do you prefer to stick to a schedule, or do you prefer to be spontaneous? Why?

A. My workday is very structured because I'm generally in four or five meetings a day. On the weekends, I like to have a plan, but not necessarily a set schedule.

That in itself is a relaxing change of pace for me, but I feel I'd be wasting time with no plan at all.

Be careful that, whichever answer you choose, it's consistent with the job you're interviewing for. For example, since accounting is a profession that requires discipline and precision, your answer should reflect your natural inclination toward agendas, schedules, and precision. However, for a sales job, you'd probably want to show that you're prepared to wing it. This question is essentially about your personality but is also about your compatibility with the job.

Q. Tell me about an interest that you outgrew.

A. Early on, I wanted to be a research physician. Then I spent time in a chemistry lab and realized I wasn't looking forward to the next two years of lab work.

That's why I've chosen marketing for medical equipment instead. It combines my respect for the medical profession with a job that's more suited to my personality.

Describe a former interest or hobby that you no longer pursue, making sure that the interest isn't related in some way to the job you're interviewing for. Talk about why you outgrew the interest and how it's not compatible with your current interests. Be sure to discuss how your current interests are related to your career.

Q. Describe a movie you've seen that really inspired you.

A. I loved one part of an otherwise depressing movie, One Flew over the Cuckoo's Nest. In one scene the nurse refuses to turn on the TV for the World Series, so Jack

Nicholson looks at the blank screen and starts narrating as though the game were actually on. The other patients gather around him and follow the game. I thought that scene was an example of the power of visualization in making things happens.

Demonstrate that you can assimilate knowledge from a wide variety of sources, including books and movies. Tell the interviewer about a specific book or movie that taught you something. Discuss how and where you've applied that knowledge.

6. Passion for the Business

Q. Why do you want to work in this industry?

A: I've always wanted to work in an industry that makes tools. One of my hobbies is home-improvement projects, so I've collected a number of saws manufactured by your company. I could be an accountant anywhere, but Yd rather work for a company whose products I trust.

Tell a story about how you first became interested in this type of work. Point out any similarities between the job you're interviewing for and your current or most recent job. Provide proof that you aren't simply shopping in this interview. Make your passion for your work a theme that you allude to continually throughout the interview.

Q. Why would you be particularly good at this business?

A: J was a pastry chef, so I understand dessert products well and can help you with new product development.

Recent preservatives have come a long way toward eliminating texture difference in pastry dough. This means we can investigate many more products than before.

Show how you keep up due to natural inquisitiveness, reading, and so on. Do you have sufficient natural interest to go that extra step and channel appropriate energy into your work? Give a specific answer.

Q. How do you stay current?

A. J pores over the Wall Street Journal, the Times, Institutional Investor, and several mutual fund newsletters. And I have a number of friends who are analysts.

Demonstrate natural interest in the industry or career field by describing publications or trade associations that are compatible with your goal.

Q. Why do you think this industry would sustain your interest over the long haul?

Al The technology in the industry is changing so rapidly that I see lots of room for job enhancement regardless of promotions. I'm particularly interested in the many applications for multimedia as a training tool.

What expectations or projections do you have for the business that would enable you to grow without necessarily advancing? What excites you about the business? What proof can you offer that your interest has already come from a deep curiosity—perhaps going back at least a few years—rather than a current whim you'll outgrow?

Q. Where do you want to be in five years?

A. I'd like to have the opportunity to work in a plant as well as at the home office. I also hope to develop my management skills, perhaps by managing a small staff.

Don't give specific time frames or job titles. Talk about what you enjoy, skills that are natural to you, realistic problems or opportunities you'd expect in your chosen field or industry, and what you hope to learn from those experiences.

You shouldn't discuss your goals in a field or industry unrelated to the job you're applying for. This may sound obvious, but too many job candidates make this mistake, unwittingly demonstrating a real lack of interest in their current field or industry. Needless to say, such gaffes wills immediately eliminate you from further consideration.

Q. Describe your ideal career.

A. I'd like to stay in afield related to training no matter what happens. I was too interested in business to work at a university, but I believe that teaching is somehow in my blood. I've been good at sales because I took the time to educate my clients. Now I look forward to training the new hires.

Talk about what you enjoy, skills that are natural to you, realistic problems or opportunities you'd expect in this particular job or industry, and what you hope to learn from those experiences. Avoid mentioning specific time frames or job titles.

Q. If you had unlimited time and financial resources, how would you spend them?

A. I'd love to be able to take several executive seminars on financial management that aren't geared toward financial experts. I'd also love to be able to shut down my department long enough to send everyone through an Outward Bound-type program. Finally, I'd probably travel and look at foreign competitors, and enjoy the food along the way. What would you do?

Although it's tempting to discuss things you'd do for fun, stick to job- or industry-related pursuits, or to skill-building efforts that could transfer to the job you're applying for. For example, if you're applying for a teaching job, you might also be interested in volunteering for an adult literacy program; this demonstrates a passion for your field—a belief in the importance of education—even without pay as an incentive.

7. Motivation and Purpose

Q. Tell me something about yourself that I didn't know from reading your resume.

A. You wouldn't know that I've managed my own small portfolio since I was sixteen, but I believe that it's important for you to understand my interest in investment sales. I've averaged a 12 percent return over the past eight years.

Don't just repeat what's on your resume. Think of a talent or skill that didn't quite fit into your employment history, but that's unique and reveals something intriguing about your personality or past experience.

Q. Tell me what you know about this company.

A. I served as an intern to a restaurant analyst last summer, so I followed all the steak-house chains closely. What you've done especially well is focus on a limited menu with great consistency among locations; the business traveller trusts your product anywhere in the U.S. I'm particularly interested in your real-estate finance group and expansion plans.

Describe your first encounter or a recent encounter with the company or its products and services. What would be particularly motivating to you about working there as opposed to working the same type of job in a different company? The recruiter will look for evidence of genuine interest and more than just surface research on the company. Reciting the annual report isn't likely to impress most recruiters, but feedback from customers and employees will.

Q. What have you learned about our company from customers, employees, or others?

A. I actually called several of the key accounts mentioned in your brochure. Two of the customers I spoke with explained why they continued to buy from you year after year. Your distribution operation is phenomenal.

Is there any service improvements you think could still be made?

Describe how your interest has grown from personal dealings with company representatives. Think creatively in preparing for job interviews. For example, prior to your job interview, speak with retailers or workers at other distribution points about the company's product line. What can they tell you? Give one or two examples of what you've learned to explain why you're interested in this company. What's the most compelling example you can describe to prove your interest?

Q. Why do you want to work here?

A. J lost a bid several years ago to your company. I realized then that products in the computer industry are becoming increasingly similar. They're so similar now, and retail prices are so competitive, that service is the best way for a company to distinguish itself from the competition. This company has the best service record of all its competitors, and I believe it will dominate the business in the long run.

Your preparation and research should become apparent here. Give one or two reasons why you're interested in the company and what in particular piqued your interest. What's the most compelling thing you can describe about your personal experience with the company its products, or its employees? Possible answers include the company's reputation, the job description itself, or a desire to get involved with the industry.

Q. What particular aspect of the company interests you most?

A. I'm most interested in your Latin American developments. My father was an army officer, so we lived for three years in Latin America. I know you've just entered joint ventures with two processing companies there. What are your plans for the next few years?

This is another opportunity for you to showcase your special knowledge of the company. If you did the proper research, as described in chapter 1, you should have no problem answering this question.

Q. What's your favourite product made by our company?

A. I've used Softer than Ever shampoo for years. In fact, my initial contact with the company was the brand manager for Softer than Ever. She encouraged me to apply for an HR position here.

Describe personal use—why do you use the company's products? What do you think are new market opportunities for that product?

Q. What do you think of our newest product and ads?

A. It seems that your new ads are trying to show that breakfast time is family time, with certain wholesomeness. Are you doing this to balance against the recent bad press about high-fat foods, without attacking the issue directly?

You should be familiar enough with the company's new products and advertising campaigns to make informed, intelligent comments about them. Offer specific suggestions and positive comments.

Q. Tell me what you think our distinctive advantage is within the industry.

A: With your low-cost-producer status and headquarters operation in a low-cost area of the country, you seem in a better position to be able to spend aggressively on R&D, even in a down year, compared to your closest rival

Describe things you believe the company does very well, particularly compared to its competition. Explain how the financial strength of the company is important.

Q. Where do you think we're the most vulnerable as a business?

A. Your cash position and strong product presence make you an attractive target for a takeover. That's my only major concern. I've already worked for one organization that merged with another, but I also know I can weather the storm.

Describe things you believe the company does not do well compared to its competition. Explain how the company's financial strength is important. If you've a passion for the business, the future of the job is probably always on your mind.

Q. What would you do differently if you ran the company?

A. I might investigate whether to sell off the light manufacturing businesses and start an aggressive supplier-relations program.

In a constructive way demonstrate that you have enough knowledge about the business to answer this question convincingly. One way to gain such knowledge is by talking to a sufficient number of company insiders, which is why this question can quickly weed out the "shoppers" from more serious job candidates. You can also turn the question around—ask for the recruiter's ideas, too. You might learn something valuable.

Q. What other firms are you interviewing with, and for what positions?

A. Actually, I've definitely decided to pursue a career as a restaurant manager, so I'm applying only for restaurant management-training programs. I've recently had interviews with several other large national fast-food chains, such as Super Burger and Clackey's Chicken.

Often the candidate will try to impress the employer by naming some large firms in unrelated industries with completely different types of jobs. This is a big mistake! What employers want to hear is that you're interviewing for similar jobs in the same industry at similar firms. This illustrates that you're committed to finding a job in your field of interest and are likely to be a low-risk hire.

Q. Do you believe you're overqualified for this position?

A. Not at all my experience and qualifications make me do my job only better, and in my opinion, my good design skills help to sell more books. My business experience helps me run the art department in a cost efficient manner, thus saving the company money.

Finally, I think I'm able to attract better freelance talent because of all my industry contacts. My qualifications are better for the company, too, since you'll be getting a better return for your investment.

Again, I'm interested in establishing a long-term relationship with my employer, and if I did well, I would expect expanded responsibilities that could make use of even other skills.

Most people don't expect to be asked if they have a great deal of experience. This question could quite easily catch a can did ate off guard, which is exactly the interviewer's intention.

The candidate doesn't hesitate in answering this question and shows complete confidence in his or her ability.

Q. Describe our competition as you see it.

A. Most of your competitors have tried to do too many things. As a result, most have had difficulty expanding and maintaining consistent quality.

Give evidence that you've researched the company and industry carefully and acquired more than superficial knowledge. Point out positive and/or negative aspects of the company's competitors. Discuss how the company's initiatives are better suited to your personal interests.

Q. What would you do if one of our competitors offered you a position?

A. I'd say no. I'm not interested in other players in this industry. I want to work for Nike because won a number of races wearing the Nike brand. Because of my positive experience with Nike, I know I'd be convincing selling your product to retailers.

The interviewer is trying to determine whether the candidate is truly interested in the industry and company, or whether he or she has chosen the company randomly.

Contrast your perceptions of the company with its competitors, and talk about the company's products or services that you've encountered. In the long run, which players do you believe are most viable and why? This is also a good place to ask the interviewer for his or her opinion.

Q. Why are you ready to leave your current job?

A. My interest lies in returning to the banking industry. I can work in human-resources management in many environments, but I believe that my experience as a lender prepares me exceptionally well for recruiting new lenders into the training program.

Give two or three reasons why you're ready to leave your current job. Focus on limitations in growth, or lack of challenge, in your current job. Make sure you point out why you believe the position you're interviewing for would provide the challenge and additional responsibilities that you desire.

Q. What do you want out of your next job?

A: I'm really interested in taking over a territory where we aren't very well positioned. My sales successes to date have been in areas where we already had a decent market share. I also want a very aggressive commission structure if I'm able to turn around a problem territory.

This question is similar to "Why are you ready to leave your current job?" Give one or two examples from your current work experience that explain why you're interviewing for the position. Focus on your desire for greater challenge. For example, "I've gone as far as I can go in my current job unless someone vacates a position." Make sure you point out why you believe the job at hand provides the additional responsibilities you're seeking.

Q. What's your dream job?

Al My dream job would include all of the responsibilities and duties in this position you're trying to fill. I also thrive in a fast-changing environment where there's business growth. Your plans call for expanding internationally during the next year, and this would satisfy one of my ultimate goals of being involved in an international corporation.

This is your ideal chance to sell your aptitudes that fit the job description. Show an interest in finding new ways these skills can be put to use in a new job with additional responsibilities. Tie in the industry, size of the company, or other factors where appropriate.

Q. What motivates you to do this kind of work?

A. I've been fortunate in my own schooling; I had wonderful teachers. I want to be that same kind of teacher—who not only encourages kids to learn but also sets an example that inspires others to want to teach. In the long run, that's our best chance of turning around the quality of education in this state.

The interviewer will want to know about your belief in the products or services of the company. Use personal experience to demonstrate your interests and strengths. In an interview for your ideal job, you'd be highly motivated to get paid for working at something you liked. The interviewer will want to know if your natural interests are compatible with this particular job.

Q. What salary would you expect for this job?

A. Based on your job description, which mentions that you prefer someone with a master's degree in engineering, I hope you consider the fact that my skills meet your highest standards. Therefore, I'd expect a salary at the high end of your pay range for the position classification. Can you give me some indication of your range?

Recruiters want to weed out people whose financial goals are unrealistic. This question is a direct hit—it forces a response about a touchy subject. If you mention a salary that's too low, you may seem uninformed; too high, and you may out price yourself or ruin your ability to bargain. It's best to turn the question back on the recruiter. Ask what the salary range is for the position; then ask the recruiter to consider how your qualifications rate compared to the average requirements for the position.

Q. What new skills or ideas do you bring to the job that other candidates aren't likely to offer?

A: Because I've worked with the oldest player in this industry, I can help you avoid some of the mistakes we made in our established markets. I think that retaining your core customer base is more important than securing new accounts right now.

This question addresses the candidate's motivation for adding "true value" to the job. Have you thought about the job carefully, considering current limitations or weaknesses in the current department and your unique abilities? If you're running neck and neck with another candidate, your ability here to prove "I offer what you need and then some" could land you the job.

Q. What interests you most about this job?

A. Yd love the opportunity to work with John Doe, whom I watched build the financial-services practice under bank deregulation. I think our utilities clients will go through a lot of the same problems that banks faced in the eighties. John's insights will be sound, and John and I have worked well together on several projects. Points out the new experiences you look forward to in the job as well as reason you believe you're uniquely suited to the position. Point out similarities to some of your past jobs in which you enjoyed success.

Q. What would you like to accomplish that you weren't able to accomplish in your last position?

A. J was hampered by a small budget that limited our marketing efforts to print ads and other traditional resources. I'd like to explore interactive media, because the eight-to-twenty-five-year-old category responds to computer-based media.

This question should be answered in the same way you'd answer "Why are you ready to leave your current job?"

Remain positive—discuss things you enjoy and have an aptitude for, but avoid dwelling on the limitations of your last job.

Q. We have a number of applicants interviewing for this position. Why should we take a closer look at you?

A. I'm probably one of the few CPAs you'll find who's worked in two Hispanic countries. With all the production that you're out sourcing to Mexico, I may be able to provide some assistance with your inventory planning.

This is similar to the question "Why should I hire you?"

What's the most compelling item you can describe to prove your qualifications and interest? Is there something extra you offer besides the basic job qualifications? Be specific in your answer. Whatever answer you prepare, try using it when you wrap up the interview, if you haven't yet been asked this question.

Q. How have your career motivations changed over the past few years?

A. When I started in sales, I didn't realize how much I'd miss it if I left. Now I want to stay close to the field organization, even though I'm looking at marketing jobs. Your firm attracts me because the account-team concept would keep me in tune with customer needs.

Describe what you've learned from your past jobs, especially where your skills and natural instincts have become apparent. Your current motivation should relate strongly to the job you're interviewing for.

Q. Why should I hire you?

A. My uncle had a company that was a small-scale manufacturer in the industry, and although he later sold the business, I worked there for five summers doing all sorts of odd jobs. For that reason I believe I know this business from the ground up, and you can be assured that I know what I'd be getting into as a plant manager here.

Don't repeat your resume or employment history. Offer one or two examples to explain why you're talking to this particular company. What's the most compelling example you can give to prove your interest? This question often remains unasked, but it's always in the back of a recruiter's mind. Even if this question isn't asked, you should find an opportunity to use your prepared response sometime during the interview, perhaps in your closing remarks.

8. Skills and Experience

Q. What are your key skills?

A. After working six years as a senior systems analyst, I've developed a number of key skills, including business modelling, process re-engineering, software package evaluation, and excellent programming skills in UNIX and C environments. I was very pleased to discover that these are the skills you're seeking. Do you want to hear about specific examples of my work?

Talk about your key skills and how you'll use them in this job. Avoid clichés or generalities.

Offer specific evidence, drawing parallels from your current or previous job to the job you're interviewing for.

Q. What sets you apart from the crowd?

A. Once I'm committed to a job or a project, I tackle it with tremendous intensity I want to learn everything I can, and my goal is to achieve results beyond the expectations of my supervisor. I guess you might say I'm very competitive and like to excel at everything do.

Your answer should communicate self-confidence, but avoid sounding arrogant. Talk about observations other people have made about your work, talents, or successes.

Q. What are your strengths?

A. My strengths are interpersonal skills, and I can usually win people over to my point of view. Also, I have good judgment about people and an intuitive sense of their talents and their ability to contribute to a given problem. These skills seem to me directly related to the job. I notice that you require three years' work experience for this job. Although my resume shows that I've only two years' experience, it doesn't show that I took two evening college courses related to my field and have been active in one of the professional societies. I also try to gain knowledge by reading the industry's trade journals. I'm certain that my combined knowledge and skill level is the equivalent of that of other people who actually do have three years' work experience. I'm also currently enrolled in a time management course; I can already see the effects of this course at work on my present job.

Describe two or three skills you have that are most relevant to the job. Avoid clichés or generalities; offer specific evidence.

Describe new ways these skills could be put to use in the new position. If you have to talk about weaknesses, be honest without shooting yourself in the foot—avoid pointing out a weakness that might be a major obstacle to landing the job.

For example, it might be wise to mention that you barely have the required work experience for the job; the interviewer has surely noticed this much, and then you can explain how you're qualified for the job nonetheless.

Q. How is your experience relevant to this job?

A. In my current job I've recently completed three reengineering projects. I gathered all the necessary market data, developed a benchmarking program, and put together a team to do the evaluation and analysis.

As a result I'm ready to tackle the major re-engineering project that you've listed as the priority of this job during the first year. In my past job I wet the liaison between the project engineering group and the instrumentation group in the testing of a new turbo engine. This experience will also help me tackle this job, which involves a close and careful working relationship between your technical group and your field-testing group.

Draw parallels from your current or previous job to the requirements of this job. A similarity that seems obvious to you may not be so obvious to the recruiter. Ask questions about the job, if necessary, to get the interviewer to accept your rationale.

Q. What skills do you think are most critical to this job?

A. The ability to evaluate all of the regulatory and competitive requirements for your new product is critical. I've had considerable experience in this area as a strategic-marketing and regulatory-policy analyst in my most recent job, and also in my first job.

Describe the immediate relevance of your past experience.

Draw parallels from your current or previous job to the requirements of this job.

Q. What skills would you like to develop in this job?

A. I'd like to develop my negotiating skills. I've had considerable experience interpreting and implementing large contracts, but I've been limited in negotiating the actual conditions, costs, and standards for a major contract. I believe this job will offer me the opportunity to be a member of a negotiating team and thereby to begin acquiring the skills necessary to lead the team.

Describe several aptitudes you haven't been able to develop fully in your current job. For example, your opportunity to manage the department might have been hindered because your supervisor plans to stay in his or her job at least five more years.

Q. If you had to stay in your current job, what would you spend more time on? Why?

A. If I stay in my current job, I'd like to gain more experience in labour negotiating. In particular, I'd like to help negotiate labour contracts, resolve grievances at the step-4 level, and prepare grievances for arbitration. My background in all other areas of human resources is strong, and I believe labour-relations experience will round out my skills so that I can have the opportunity to move up as a department head or a vice president in the future.

What interests you most about your job? Describe the responsibilities that give you the most satisfaction. In addition, show a real interest in upgrading the job, staying on the leading edge, and so on.

Q. How could you enrich your current job?

A. When I was a research assistant for the cable and wireless company back in ninety-three, at a time when we were experiencing rapid growth, our pricing analyst abruptly resigned for a better job. During the search to fill his position, I volunteered to help out with one of the major government projects. I worked considerable overtime, studied on my own, and helped bring the project to conclusion. I was commended for my effort and was told I'd be in line for the next opening in the pricing group.

Show an ability to add value continually to your job. What new opportunities exist that could challenge your skills and intellect? The interviewer will want to feel confident that you won't get bored or disenchanted with your work.

Q. How do you explain your job successes?

A: I never assume our customers are satisfied with our product, so I do my best to follow up with every customer. This feedback has provided valuable insight into the quality and characteristics of our products.

The customer, as well, always appreciates this follow up, especially when something hasn't gone right and you still have the opportunity to correct it on a timely basis. In addition, I'm able to pass on information to our design and production units to help improve both process and product.

Be candid without sounding arrogant. Mention observations other people have made about your work strengths or talents. This question is similar to the question "What sets you apart from the crowd?"

Q. Compared to others with a similar background in your field, how would you rate yourself?

Al I've been consistently ranked in the top 10 percent nationally for all salespeople in my field. I sell advertising space for a national news publication. My clients are primarily large ad agencies that represent corporate America. I've always enjoyed the challenge of selling to advertising-agency executives because they always set high standards and really know our product well. This brings out the very best in my competitive nature, and I'm consistently at the top, both within my publishing company and within the industry.

Be honest and self-confident without sounding arrogant.

Give clear, convincing reasons for your answer. If you've been in the top 10 percent in sales nationally, this is a good time to bring it up!

Q. How good are your writing abilities?

A. I really concentrated on further developing my writing skills while I got my M.B.A. I took an entrepreneurial class in which the chief assignment was developing, writing, and continually rewriting a very involved business plan.

This is an excellent answer. Have a business plan or something similar ready to show the recruiter. Leave your business plan with the recruiter after the interview. The recruiter will be looking for a candidate with writing ability, especially for jobs where a lot of writing is required, like for financial analysts or copywriters.

Q. What computer systems and software do you know?

A. I've used PCs with general-office software such as Microsoft Word for Windows, Word Perfect, Lotus 1-2-3, and Excel. I have some experience with Macintosh systems as well. And through my search for a computer network, I've gained some familiarity with local networks; the computer company we used trained me on basic troubleshooting issues.

In today's business environment, computer literacy is a must. Word-processing and spreadsheet experience is essential, and familiarity with database management or graphics programs is valuable as well. Most businesses use PC-compatible computers, but many companies in the creative field, such as publishing or advertising, use Macintosh computers. If you're interviewing in one of those fields, you might find it helpful to familiarize yourself with Macs.

9. Diligence and Professionalism

Q. Give an example of how you saw a project through, despite obstacles.

A. J actually rotated off an account but kept my hand in it as an adviser, because the client had threatened to pull the account if he wasn't dealing with me. Over three months I was able to make the client more comfortable with my replacement while I slowly decreased my presence.

Demonstrate how you gather resources and foresee and manage obstacles. Focus your answer on the solution and execution, not on the obstacles themselves.

Q. Share an example of your determination.

A. I led an effort to change our production system over to dedicated lines. The biggest problem wets convincing the factory workers that this strategy made sense, even though they'd have to learn to do their jobs differently. I assured them that within a few months their jobs would be easier, and we'd save about four man-hours per employee per week. I convinced management to increase the profit-sharing account using half of those savings, which also helped get the employees on my side.

Describe a time you persevered to accomplish a goal. A personal goal (for example, one that reflects an interest in developing a new skill) would be appropriate here. Demonstrate how you gather resources, predict obstacles, and manage stress.

Q. Share an example of your diligence or perseverance.

A. About halfway through our last system installation, the client changed her requirements. Our partner agreed that, at the new costs the client would incur, we could still meet the original completion date. It took about seventy to eighty hours a week for us to get the job done, but we did it, knowing that it would be over within three months.

Describe your professional character, including thoroughness, diligence, and accountability. Demonstrate how you gather resources, use time-management techniques, or go the extra mile. Use a specific example.

Q. Describe a time when you tackled a tough or unpopular assignment.

A. I had to determine which budgets would be cut within my division to yield an overall 5 percent cost reduction. I tried to remain objective and keep the personalities of department heads out of the decision.

Ultimately, I ended up getting each department head to commit to a .25 percent reduction through frugal travel-expense planning, which was an enormous part of our sales division's costs. We accomplished most of the savings by combining trips and by securing two week-advance airline reservations whenever possible.

Describe a time you were willing, or even volunteered, to solve a problem that had remained unresolved after earlier attempts. Or describe something you accomplished that was important to the company's long-term interests, even if short-term implications were less than favourable. Your answer might involve a problem employee or a process-improvement plan, for example.

Q. Would your current boss describe you as the kind of employee who goes the extra mile?

A: Absolutely. In fact, on my annual evaluations she writes that I'm the most dependable and flexible person on her staff. I think this is mostly because of my ability to juggle and prioritize. Would you like an example?

Be ready to offer proof that you persevere to see important projects through and to achieve important results. Share an example that demonstrates your dependability or willingness to tackle a tough project. If you describe "long hours of work make sure you demonstrate that the hours were productive, and not the result of poor time management.

Q. How many days were you absent from work last year? Why?

A. I was absent four days last year, three because I came down with the flu, and one due to the death of a family member.

A history of absenteeism or tardiness, or any indication of a weak work ethic or poor performance standards, can be detrimental to you. Convince the interviewer of your willingness to take responsibility at work, and of your punctuality, dependability, and solid attendance record. If you think you may get poor references because of attendance or undependability, you'd better be well prepared to give a detailed and exonerating explanation. A similar question you may be asked is 'Are you punctual?"

Q. Tell me about a time you didn't perform to your capabilities.

A. The first time I had to give a presentation to our board, I failed to anticipate some of their questions. I was unprepared for anything other than what I wanted to report. Now my director and I brainstorm all the what-ifs in advance.

This question forces the candidate to describe a negative situation. Do so in the context of an early career mistake based on inexperience; then demonstrate the better judgment you now have as a result of that learning experience.

Q. Employees tend to be either concept oriented or task oriented. How do you describe yourself?

A. It's important for me to have clear direction on each project. That's why I'm good in support roles, with managers who have very specific ideas. I'm thorough at carrying out the tasks.

With this question the interviewer looks for a match between the candidate's preferred level of detail and the level of detail required by the job. Problems might arise if the job requires delegation but the candidate enjoys working independently. When you've completed projects in the past, have you performed within the scope of the task assigned?

Q. What would your colleagues tell me about your attention to detail?

A. My co-workers always count on me to help them think through what might have been overlooked, so they'd probably tell you I think through processes from A to Z

Here the interviewer is interested in the candidate's depend ability and follow-through. Are you responsible? Have you contributed productively to a team effort without getting caught up in unnecessary detail? Do you use your time efficiently? Do you mention specific praise given by one of your peers?

Q. How do you manage stress in your daily work?

A. I try to get out for lunch at least once during the week to clear my head. I also have a personal rule that stops me from reacting to any problem until I feel calm about it. I think, and then act—but I've learned to do that over time.

It might be helpful here to describe a stressful project you've worked on and the specific actions you took to organize each step and see the project through. How do you keep yourself calm and professional under pressure?

Q. How do you regroup when things haven't gone as planned?

A: I start by trying to imagine the worst possible outcome; then I back up and identify precautions I can take to avoid that scenario. In this way I usually end up with a result close to the original goal. The training example I described earlier is proof of that skill.

Describe a time when some obstacle forced you to change your original plan, but you were still able to achieve the desired result. Did you rally the support of others to make this happen? With hindsight, how might you have better predicted the obstacle?

Q. How have you prioritized or juggled your work load in your current job?

A. I juggle by working only on my two major accounts early in the day. That way, if interruptions occur, my most critical customers are taken care of.

Demonstrate how you gather resources, how you predict obstacles, and how you manage stress. Describe personal habits that allow you to move ahead on priorities and avoid micro-managing or putting out fires. In what ways have you become better at managing time over the years?

Q. Describe a professional skill you've developed in your most recent job.

A. I'm most proud of my new skills in applying database technology—for example, in our mailing services.

What used to take us days of manual sorting now takes five minutes through a quick-search feature?

Describe a skill you've improved in order to manage your work more efficiently Typical examples might include learning a new software application, taking a professional seminar, or taking adult-education classes.

Q. Why is service such an important issue?

A. Service is a major contributor to customer satisfaction.

Just important as, or may be even more important than, cost. If a customer isn't receiving a level of service that meets or exceeds his or her expectations, that customer won't be a customer for very long. In addition, that customer's experience with your company may affect how potential customers in the marketplace view your company. People do talk and share information. This may affect not only profits but future sales as well. In many instances service may be the one thing that distinguishes a company from the competition. A bad reputation for service may compromise a company's position in the marketplace.

The interviewer is trying to determine if the candidate understands the importance of customer service in establishing a positive image in the marketplace, and its impact on new business sales. Outstanding customer service is also a great help in establishing long-term clients and repeat business—the profitable company's bread and butter. The longer is the relationship, the greater the possibility for profit.

Q. Tell me about a time when you had to deal with an irate customer. How did you handle the situation?

Al My customer service position at the telephone company involved dealing occasionally with irate customers.

When that happened, I'd try to talk in calm, even voice, in order to get the person to respond in a businesslike manner and focus on trying to resolve the situation. Most times I was able to rectify the problem and pacify the customer, but I remember one incident in particular in which the caller became verbally abusive. I tried to remain calm and professional and not to let my personal feelings enter into the situation. I didn't respond to the abuse, I just made a note of it and continued to help the customer as best I could.

When the abuse persisted, however, I politely asked him to call back and ask for my manager, because at that point I knew I couldn't resolve the problem.

How you react when others lose their temper or become upset is very important in most positions, especially in service industries. The interviewer will be looking for evidence of your aptitude for work that involves a great deal of contact with the public. Give an example of a time when you were faced with a difficult person and how you handled it. Your answer should illustrate your maturity, diplomacy, and awareness of the needs and feelings of others.

Q. Are there any issues from your personal life that might potentially have an impact on your professional career?

A. I'm always careful to separate my personal life from my professional life. I believe it's important to remain objective when treating patients. A therapist should always be able to take an emotional step back in order to make an unbiased assessment of a patient. It only hurts the patient when you try to project your own issues and feelings onto that patient.

This question is especially important to those in the health service fields. The interviewer wants to determine how well you've integrated yourself as an individual. If you have personal issues that you've been unable to work through, they could easily interfere with your relationships with your patients. These issues could also affect your judgment in assessing patients, as well as how you approach treatment planning and recommendations. Assure the interviewer that you can sort out personal opinions from professional behaviour. For instance, if you've experienced a crisis that you haven't dealt with positively, you might not be willing to help your patients face really traumatic issues because that would bring up too many of your own intense emotions.

Q. When have your skills in diplomacy been put to the test?

A. A customer came in once and demanded money back for an evening dress that had apparently been worn.

She claimed it was a different colour after dry cleaning and that the cleaner said the fabric was faulty. I quickly told her we'd happily return her money, even though I didn't think she was being honest I decided it was more important to keep other customers from hearing her and maybe doubting our high-quality merchandise.

Describe a problem situation with a client or a work associate that you resolved by remaining objective. How did you show empathy and build rapport?

Q. How do you manage your work week and make realistic deadlines?

A. I always reserve two hours of dead time every day to handle any unanticipated problems that may occur. I used to plan for eight or nine hours of project time, but now I find that I'm able to manage my own projects, as well as whatever my boss and staff need from me.

To answer this question effectively, describe in detail how you establish priorities, set deadlines, and determine schedules.

Q. Tell me about a time you had to extend a deadline.

A. Two weeks into a job, it was clear that our client expected us to add more features ets we

went along. I renegotiated with the client, outlined his goals, and showed him a price structure similar to a menu, from which he could choose more features at a higher cost and in a longer timeframe. He opted for something in the middle that he understood would cause a three week adjustment to the schedule.

Describe your accountability and willingness to adjust a deadline in order to satisfy the overall goals of a project. Had you not adjusted the deadline, what goal would have been compromised?

Q. What personal skill or work habit have you struggled to improve?

A. I had to learn to say no. I used to be helpful to the point that other staff abused my goodwill. Now I offer to help by countering with something I'd like help on in return. On balance I believe the trade-off is more equitable, and cooperation in our office has improved over time.

This question is similar to "Describe a professional skill you've developed in your most recent job." However, here you probably want to discuss an improvement from the earliest days of your career or from your relatively distant past. Make sure you convince the interviewer that this particular work habit is no longer an obstacle.

Q. What books do you keep on your desk?

A. I keep a good dictionary on my desk. I also keep Strunk and White, which is a good reference for looking up all the grammar rules that you learned in high school and college but forgot, or for particularly difficult situations.

The recruiter will be interested in determining how seriously you take your profession. A good dictionary and a good reference book are typical, and necessary, books for a writer to keep on hand. Perhaps you like to keep your favourite novel on your desk as well.

10. Creativity and Leadership

Q. What colour is your brain?

A. My brain is red because I'm always hot. I'm always on fire with new plans and ideas. Be aware that you'll probably be asked zany questions. The point is not to stump you, but to find out what makes you tick. When the standard interview questions are asked, people are prepared, and it's harder for the recruiter to get to know the real person. An advertising recruiter, for example, tries to avoid this. There is no right or wrong answer to this type of question. In fact, the recruiter won't even really care what your answer is. He or she just doesn't want to hear something like, 'T don't know, I guess it's blue because that's the way I imagine it." The point is to see how creative you are and how you think. Be sure to explain why you answered the way that you did.

Q. If you got on an elevator where everyone was facing the back, what would you do?

A. I think I'd face the front anyway and say aloud, "It's really much more comfortable facing forward, you know."

Interviews in creative fields like advertising and graphic design are different from other types of job interviews.

Advertising recruiters tend to have a different interview style and process, usually conducting more of a behavioural inters view. Recruiters ask questions like these to figure out what your behaviour might be in a particular real-life situation.

Q. What's the most creative or innovative project you've worked on?

A. During my summer job at Cellular One, I noticed that the sales inquiries were distributed haphazardly to all the marketing assistants in the office. I decided to set up a system grouping inquiries according to region or according to company size. This approach enabled the entire marketing team to come up with better and more creative solutions to our sales problems.

Provide examples of your initiative and resourcefulness.

Discuss how your leadership skills have helped you accomplish your goals. Give a specific example that shows a creative, new, or unusual approach to reaching your goals.

Q. Describe a time when you've creatively overcome an obstacle.

A. My publishing company could never get an appointment with a major Fortune 500 company.

After several sales representatives gave up in frustration, I volunteered to take a crack at the account. Instead of contacting the vice president of advertising, I decided to target the VP's administrative assistant. I scheduled an appointment with the assistant and gave him my sales pitch. I really made an impression, because the assistant convinced the vice president that she should schedule an appointment with me. In fact, she pencilled me in on her calendar on the spot. I had the appointment, and we got the order two weeks later.

In answer to this question, it's often helpful to focus on how you overcome problems by rallying the support of your co-workers. How have you approached a problem differently from how others might have addressed the same problem?

Emphasize your creative solution and its positive results.

Q. Consider the following scenario: You're working late one evening and are the last person in the office. You answer an urgent telephone call to your supervisor from a sales rep who's currently meeting with a potential client. The sales rep needs an answer to a question to close the sale. Tomorrow will be too late. You have the expertise to answer the question, but it's beyond your normal level of authority. How would you respond?

A. I'd get all the pertinent information, taking well documented notes. I'd then answer the question based on my knowledge and the information provided. I'd leave my supervisor a note and fill him or her in on the details the next morning. I'd be sure to explain my decision, as well as the thought process behind it.

This response shows that the candidate is confident in his or her ability and can be counted on in an emergency.

Similarly, your answer should indicate that you're not afraid to be the decision maker in a tough situation, even if the situation's beyond your normal level of authority.

Q. Why do you think that some companies with good products fail?

A. Employees who are involved in the design and/or manufacture of a product must totally understand and believe in the product and use it on a regular basis. Only in this way can they continually modify and improve it to the customer's satisfaction. Any product must be constantly fine-tuned to meet the changing needs and demands of the consumer. Only by getting the employees involved with the product and excited about it can this improvement occur.

This is a question about the candidate's vision as a leader. If you're asked this question, you'll do well to discuss a specific example of a product or idea that failed because of poor enthusiasm from employees or other consumers. Without being overly critical, you should discuss what you would have done differently.

Q. How resourceful are you?

A. At one time, for all of our new product launches, our Chief engineer would release a press statement about its virtues. But when I was given responsibility for a new launch, I decided to get three of our largest customers to videotape an endorsement for use in our marketing campaign. The result was a far higher level of credibility, and we exceeded our six-month sales quota.

We now use personal endorsements routinely when we launch our products.

This is a question about the candidate's creativity and initiative. Provide an example of how you've changed your plan or direction and achieved the same, or a better, result. You might want to focus on how you obtained crucial information or how you changed your personal style to get someone to cooperate.

Q. Give me proof of your persuasiveness.

A. During my summer internship I was assigned the task of conducting a benchmarking study for all the communication expenditures for a major utility. I had to get the consensus of employees in several different departments. Unfortunately, they resented the fact that I was just a summer intern, and they refused to cooperate. I had to schedule individual meetings with every employee and persuade each one that what I was doing would be ultimately beneficial to his or her own department and to the company. After a frustrating month I finally got everyone's cooperation, the project went flawlessly, and in the end I received a bonus for my efforts.

This is a question about leadership, but tries not to use an example in which you were the designated leader. If possible, describe a time when you didn't really have authority but instead used your powers of persuasion to get people on your side. Describe your goal and the outcome of your efforts.

Why did people trust or believe you?

Q. What would your last supervisor say about your initiative?

A: In any job I hold I can usually find inefficiencies in a process, and I always try to take some initiative to come up with a solution for improvement. My last supervisor was a little surprised and flustered the first few months when I was constantly coming to him with my ideas for improvements. He finally accepted the fact that I had some good ideas and encouraged me to write up in a proposal every month my one best idea so that he could get me the resources to tackle the solution on a formal basis. My first big project had to do with improving the inventory control in one of our manufacturing shops. Because the records for inventory receivable were inconsistent, I set up an entirely new inventory-order system and used that data to trace the history of the inventory—for example, when it was used, how it wets used, and my recommendations for necessary replacement. I reduced the total value of the inventory we had to carry by 23 percent the first year. As a result, my supervisor would always use me as an example of someone who's constantly taking the initiative.

Describe a project you volunteered to work on to solve an existing problem or to avoid a potential problem. How did you approach your supervisor with the idea initially? Focus on the creativity of the idea, your approach, and the result you obtained.

Q. Describe an improvement you personally initiated.

A. J improved the inventory-management system for all laboratory supplies and equipment in a department of medicine at the university where I previously worked.

The system was one that had been handed down year after year, and no one had ever bothered to question its efficiency. I decided we needed a whole new system, and I took it upon myself to design and implement one.

This required several extra hours of work after my routine duties were completed, but I felt good about making this additional contribution to our department.

Give proof of your effectiveness, dedication to the job, and ability to "think outside of the box."

Q. Describe a time in your work experience when the existing process didn't work, and what you did about it.

A. The order-entry system at the telecommunications company where I worked was a mess. Orders weren't being processed properly or in a timely manner. I did a work-flow analysis to identify the bottlenecks, and then I convinced my boss that we needed to spend one hundred thousand dollars on a totally new system. He reluctantly agreed, but with the caveat that "This had better save us money." After one year, the project had paid for the investment twofold.

The interviewer wants to know what initiatives this candidate took to change a faulty process in a creative way. Show that you can approach a problem creatively and manage a situation that isn't working. Did you achieve the result you needed?

Q. Describe a time you had to alter your leadership style.

A. I'm normally a strong leader who has good vision and enjoys delegating, but I expect my orders to be carried out promptly. When I was assigned a project to increase our product exports and was given a committee of nine people to work with, I immediately assumed I had the best plan and began my normal routine of delegating. I quickly realized, though, that this group of employees, with international backgrounds, wasn't responding well. In fact, they asked to have input into my plan. I agreed to spend half a day talking with them, and then I realized that they, too, had good ideas. The only way to move ahead on the project was to encourage the entire group to offer solutions to our export problem. I think these people would agree that I'm flexible and willing to modify my leadership style when the need arises.

Your answer to this question should emphasize your ability to make different kinds of people feel comfortable, so that a reasonable working relationship results. Be specific. What initiatives did you take to improve a less-than-ideal situation?

What would the other people involved say about you now?

Q. Tell me about a good process that you made even better.

Al Recently, when I started a new job at a manufacturing company, the processes in place were very efficient and effective. However, soon after beginning the job, I was told I'd have to reduce the budget by 20 percent. The only way to do this while maintaining the current workload was to make the processes even more efficient. I called my team together and issued a challenge that we had to take these already good processes and make them even better in order to meet the corporate objective. We exceeded even our own expectations and showed that any process can be improved, with critical evaluation and creative thinking.

The interviewer wants specific examples of how the candidate has added value, even when an existing situation was already good. In response to a question like this, prove you're creative enough to bring a new level of quality to the job. Can you demonstrate the value you've added in every past job?

Q. Tell me about a time you persuaded others to adopt your idea.

A. Our customer retention at the biotech company where I worked was poor. I thought we could understand and improve this situation by conducting a thorough customer-attitude survey. My boss thought this would be a waste of time, but I finally persuaded him that we could uncover some of the core reasons why retention had been getting progressively worse. I showed him how our competitors had been using customer surveys to their advantage. He agreed, and the surveys were used to make a number of changes in how we dealt with customers. For example, the survey revealed that customers were frustrated at not being able to quickly get through to the order-entry department—that the phone would often ring five or six times before someone would answer it. As one of the new supervisors, I started grabbing the phone on the first ring and helping to process the order. My initiative was noticed, and a few other supervisors started pitching in and doing the same thing. Before long, everyone was involved in answering the phone when we had an overload of incoming calls. This not only improved the efficiency of our order-entry process but caused all of the workers to take note that the supervisors truly were involved and interested in the department. Their efficiency also began to improve.

Emphasize here your ability to rally support and to make people comfortable with your ideas. Be specific. This question is common in interviews for sales positions.

Q. How would a former colleague or subordinate describe your leadership style?

A. My colleagues would probably say that my leadership style is the strong, silent type. I don't make a big deal about being in charge or making decisions. I try to involve everyone around me in the decision-making process and in carrying out a plan of action. My colleagues truly believe that I bring a lot of positive energy to our group and that I help motivate others.

The interviewer is trying to determine what the candidate's references or colleagues will say if they're called. Be objective and realistic without embellishing or being overly modest.

Describe candidly your leadership style, giving specific examples that reflect your personal approach. Would former colleagues describe your contributions as generally positive for the department?

Q. Do you believe that your job appraisals have adequately portrayed your leadership abilities?

A. Although I had limited opportunity to demonstrate my leadership abilities in my previous job, I'm certain my appraisals would mention that I'm extremely thorough and dependable with my assignments. I take the time to make sure that all those around me clearly understand what our objectives are. This quality has enabled me to gain the confidence and respect of my co-workers and has been mentioned by my supervisor during performance appraisals.

This question is especially important if an outcome in your past work experience wasn't positive despite your efforts, or if you haven't had an opportunity to play a real leadership role.

Q. Describe the situations in which you're most comfortable as a leader.

A. One of my talents is to take complex issues or problems and break them down into their simplest parts. I'm also good at teaching other people. As a result, whenever I'm faced with a complex problem, other people tend to let me find a solution and instruct them on how to proceed. As a result, I've found that I'm an effective leader in this kind of situation. I'm not a particularly effective leader, though, in a highly charged political environment. My preference is to deal with facts and data. When there are other issues like political or emotional factors to consider, I often prefer that someone else take the lead, and I simply resolve to be a good team player. In all other situations I normally surface as a leader.

Describe situations in which you've had experience as a creative leader and people have trusted you. Why do people tend to follow your lead in these situations? This is more an issue of earned authority than of outright authority. Conversely if you're asked to describe situations in which you're a better contributor than leader, you can define types of problems that you're less comfortable working on or situations in which you feel you're too opinionated or biased to lead without con trolling the group unfairly. Then end by describing instances when you've played the leader well.

Q. Describe your comfort level working with people of higher rank and people of lower rank.

Al The person that delivers our mail twice a day has become a good friend. I've invited him to my house to meet my family, and we'll often go to baseball games together on the weekends. I can also relate well to my general manager. We both have common interests, which include sailing, and elk hunting in the winter.

Be specific here. Tell the interviewer how you've developed a style that's worked with a variety of people.

11. Compatibility with the Job

Q. What were the most rewarding aspects of your most recent job?

Al My favourite aspect of being a recruiter is the feeling of accomplishment you get when you know you've made a good match. I always make periodic checks on the recent recruits and their managers. Positive progress reports keep me motivated.

The interviewer is interested in how well suited the candidate is to the job. What do you do particularly well and want to do more of in your next position? Conclude by focusing on the new experiences you're seeking in your career. Your response should correspond closely to the position you're applying for.

Q. What are the limitations of your current job?

A. My job now is limited because the industry's simply not in a growth mode. Actually, that's why I became skilled in defensive marketing—retaining customers through customer-satisfaction programs that enhance our reputation and give us an edge over the competition.

Briefly explain one or two reasons why your current position doesn't allow for the growth you desire. Think about the question "Why are you ready to leave your current job?"

Above all, remain positive, focusing on what you do well and want to emphasize in your work.

Q. What do you want to achieve in your next job?

Al I hope to be able to move into finance in a manufacturing group, since I started at the home office. I think that's important to my overall understanding of the company's core business.

Your answer should describe your ideal job. Focus on what you seek in your next job, taking care that your response closely matches the position you're applying for. Wherever you're unsure, ask questions of the interviewer—for example,

"In this job would there be an opportunity to . . . ?"

Q. Describe your ideal job.

A; My ideal job would combine a sales territory that I managed and additional responsibility for sales training, so I could use my teaching background.

This question is similar to the previous one. Whatever response you prepare, make sure that it closely matches the position you're applying for.

Q. What interests you most about this job?

A. I was excited to watch your successful acquisitions in South America. Because of my exchange-program experience there, I believe I could help in your Latin American marketing effort.

Describe your qualifications for the job and how well the job fits your natural skills and abilities. Give evidence that you've performed well in similar work. What proof can you offer that you'll excel in this job?

Q. What interests you least about this job?

A. One of the things I hope not to do is prospect extensively by meeting one on one with small-account representatives. I found in my last sales territory that

I gave superior service to my major accounts by focusing my on-site time with them. I was able to grow my key account business 20 percent.

You might want to ask the interviewer, "What did the last person in the job find difficult about the position?" Whatever the answer, respond appropriately, then describe what interests you most about the job.

Q. What aspects of this job do you feel most confident about?

A; I believe that I can engage an audience really effectively when I get up in front of a room to present a new idea, I can usually get people on my side rather quickly.

Sell what you do best, and try to match it to the tasks you know are part of the job. Ask the interviewer if your skills might have been helpful in some recent project. Try to convince the interviewer that what you have to offer is truly in demand at the company in this job, in the industry.

Q. What concerns you most about performing this job?

A. My clinical experience gives me confidence that I can perform the job. Other than the fact that I've not formally managed an outpatient clinic, I'm worried about whether the support staffs is readily available to answer the phones. To get the results you want with your hot line, staff will have to be available at all times to answer questions about our services.

You may want to turn the question around; ask the inter viewer if he or she has any concerns about your qualifications.

Then address those concerns and affirm your confidence that your skills are the right ones and your interests are compatible with the position. Offer proof that will dispel any doubts the interviewer may have.

Q. What skills do you offer that are most relevant to this job?

A: My engineering background gives me a logical problem-solving ability that I know will be useful in assessing client needs. That background will also help your consulting firm sell business to manufacturers who themselves employ many engineers.

Your answer should be similar to your prepared response to the question "What interests you most about this job?" Use examples to back up the most relevant information from your resume.

Q. Considering your own resume, what are your weaknesses in relation to this job?

A: What are you most concerned about? If you're worried about my sincerity in working for a non-profit organization, I hope that my discussion about my family's philanthropic efforts has made you more comfortable with my motives.

The best approach here is to turn the question around and get the interviewer to disclose what he or she believes are your weaknesses. Then use the opportunity to change the inter viewer's mind. As always, give specific examples of your suit ability for the position.

Q. How did the realities differ from your expectations in your last job?

A. The hardest thing to foresee was how other departments within the company would view my market-research department's work. Unfortunately, I found that many groups prefer to go outside for specialized research services, and that's really the reason I decided to contact your firm.

The interviewer is trying to determine if, in the past, the candidate was realistic about judging his or her suitability for a job. If, for the most part, you've been a pretty good judge of such things, you've probably screened yourself carefully for this job. The recruiter also wants to ensure that any past disenchantment won't be repeated in this job.

Q. How would you enrich your current job?

A. I will decide to stay with my current job, I'm going to volunteer to be on the communications taskforce, which is trying to get all of our offices linked to the Internet and other resources.

Without dwelling on the negatives, describe how you've improved the quality of your job so that you've continued to develop your skills and enjoy your work. Don't give the interviewer the impression that, if dissatisfied, you're unable to work on a solution or a plan for improvement.

Conclude by focusing on the qualities you seek in your next job. Your response should correspond closely to the description of the position you're applying for.

Q. Would you be able to travel as necessary to perform the job?

A. I will have adequate notice; I can arrange to be available for travel at almost any time of the year. As it is, I usually travel about once a month for my current job.

Your response should be consistent with the demands of the position you're currently applying for, reflecting a realistic understanding of the work and time required. Inquire about seasonality of work, if you're unsure, and show a willingness to spend extended hours periodically.

Q. Why is this particularly good job for someone with your qualifications?

A. Based on what you've told me about the last person who excelled in this job, I'm confident that I've the same skills in spreadsheet analysis and statistics. I'd also work well with your audit team, because I come from that kind of environment and know what a client can do to make the consulting relationship more productive.

The best answer here will describe positive experiences and results of recent jobs that were comparable to this one.

Q. What's your most productive or ideal work setting?

A. I like having at least one hour of uninterrupted time in the early morning to plan my day. I usually start around 7 a.m. Otherwise, I enjoy an office with open doors, constant feedback, and lots of energy and activity. It helps me work more productively when I sense how busy everyone else is, too.

The interviewer wants to know the impact that the candidate's working environment has on his or her job performance. How well would you fit the position, physical layout of the department, and attitudes of the particular work group?

Emphasize your ability to work in a variety of settings and how you've managed to be productive in less-than-ideal work environments.

Q. Do you prefer continuity in structure or frequent change in your daily work?

A. I enjoy change and challenge, which is why I frequently ask for the tough assignments. The last two projects we discussed were ones that I asked for. I don't allow myself to get bored.

Your answer should be consistent with the job description.

Describe environments that have allowed you to remain interested and learn new things without getting bored.

12. Personality and Cultural Compatibility

Q. What would your friends tell me about you?

A. My friends would tell you that I move faster than most people, eat more than most people, work later than most people, and still manage to spend time with friends despite my schedule. I believe in doing lots of things with gusto.

Talk about parts of your personality that will naturally be revealed on the job.

Q. Tell me about your relationship with your previous bosses.

A. My bosses would tell you that I've often acted as a sounding board for them. With all three of my bosses, we've mentored each other, although the obvious balance of wisdom and expertise was theirs. I was always helpful to them in their decisions about customer problems.

The interviewer is interested in whether the candidate and the supervisor for the position will work well together. As you describe each previous boss, the interviewer will most likely be making mental comparisons to the supervisor. The inter viewer must feel confident that he or she has uncovered any surprises about your working relationships, and that you won't end up clashing with your new boss. Try to be honest without being negative. Emphasize the type of boss you work well with.

Q. Describe your working relationship with your colleagues.

A. They'd probably tell you that nothing ever shocks me or sets me back too much, and that I'm really an asset as an adviser when they suffer a roadblock, as in the case we discussed about the contractor. I'm constant and dependable.

What types of people do you enjoy working with? How would the company's customers or clients react to you? From your answer the interviewer must feel confident that any surprises about your work personality have been uncovered. Give examples of how you pitched in, how you know to ask for help when you need it, and your concern for the group's accomplishments.

Q. Describe your personality beneath the professional image.

A. I laugh a lot at my own shortcomings. I see irony in most things and I'm outspoken, but I bring a sense of humour to any office. I think it provides a nice balance of warmth in a work setting.

This is similar to the question "What would your friends tell me about you?" Concentrate on how your personality reflects your job skills or interests.

CHAPTER 7

50 Smashes!

One of the biggest fears that job candidates harbour about interviews is the unanticipated question for which they have no answer. To make matters worse, some recruiters may ask a question knowing full well that you can't possibly answer it. These types of questions are known as stress questions and are designed for their shock effect.

Sometimes recruiters ask stress questions not because they enjoy seeing you squirm in your seat, but because they want to judge how well you might react to pressure or tension on the job.

If you encounter a stress question, your best bet is to stay calm, diplomatic, and positive in your response. Don't get defensive or allow your confidence to be shaken, and try to answer the question to the best of your ability. If you simply can't answer the question, think about it for a few seconds.

Then, with a confident smile and without apology, simply say, "I can't answer that question."

Following are fifty of the most challenging questions you'll ever face. If you're able to answer these questions, you'll be prepared to handle just about anything the recruiter comes up with.

Q. Time management has become a necessary factor in productivity. Give an example of a time-management skill you've learned and applied at work.

A. I regularly use scheduling software, which helps me effectively plan for the day, week, month, or year. It also has a to-do-list feature and an alarm option, which is helpful for meeting timely deadlines. In general, though, I'm very goal oriented and self disciplined.

I like to focus clearly on one project at a time for a set amount of hours. In the past I've found that this has helped me save time, which in turn has given me the opportunity to implement new procedures that have ultimately saved the department time and money.

When answering this question, describe a time-management technique you've applied at work that's allowed you to save time and resources. In such areas as public relations time is precious, and the interviewer will want to see that you have an idea of how valuable your time is. Try to give an example that demonstrates how you've managed to increase productivity because of effective time management.

Q. How do you handle tension with your boss?

A. The only tension I've ever felt was once when we both got too busy to keep each other informed. My boss overcommitted me with a short deadline, not knowing that I was bogged down with another client problem. I believe firmly in the importance of staff meetings so that co-workers can respect the demands on each other's time.

The safest ground here is to describe an example of a miscommunication in your early relationship with a boss and how you resolved it. The interviewer will want to know how you avoided a recurrence of the problem.

Q. What would you say are the broad responsibilities of an editorial assistant?

A. Though I'm sure it varies from company to company, I think it would be safe to say that being an editorial assistant involves a lot of typing, filing, and general administrative work. I would probably be expected to read and evaluate book proposals, write manuscript rejection letters have some limited correspondence with authors, and generally assist the editor in whatever needed to be done.

You will probably be asked this question in some form or another. This question is similar to "How did the realities differ from your expectations in your last job?" but a little more subtle. Although both questions are basically trying to deter mine the same thing, this version is a little trickier. Many entry-level applicants have a "glamorized" view of their industry and are unhappily surprised to find themselves per forming mundane, clerical tasks. The employer wants to make sure that you have a realistic view of the job and will be likely to be happy in that position for several years.

Q. What is your current salary?

A. I currently earn an annual salary of thirty-five thousand dollars with full benefits.

By all means, if you're asked about your salary history, don't embellish. More and more companies are starting to verify applicants' pay history, some even demanding to see W-2 forms from job seekers. If you get the job, a falsehood discovered even years later may be grounds for immediate dismissal.

Don't leave yourself open to this kind of trouble.

Q. Would you be willing to relocate to another city?

A. I'd prefer to be based here, but it's certainly a possibility I'd be willing to consider.

You may, even in some first interviews, be asked questions that seem to elicit a tremendous commitment on your behalf, such as this one. Although such questions may be unfair during an initial job interview, you may well conclude that you have nothing to gain and everything to lose with a negative response. If you're asked such a question unexpectedly during an initial job interview, simply say something like "That's certainly a possibility" or "I'm willing to consider that."

Later, if you receive an offer, you can find out the specific work conditions and then decide if you wish to accept the position. Remember, at the job-offer stage you have the most negotiating power, and the employer may be willing to accommodate your needs. If that isn't the case, you might wish to explain that upon reflection, you've decided you can't relocate but you'd like to be considered for other positions that might open up in the future.

Q. Does the frequent travel required for this work fit into your lifestyle?

A. The frequent travel in this consulting position is no problem for me or my family. My wife is an airline flight attendant, so neither of us follows the typical nine-to-five routine.

If you're comfortable divulging information about your family situation, now is the time to do so. The interviewer is concerned here that the candidate may not be able to travel as much as the job requires. Emphasize your flexibility, or explain why travel wouldn't be a problem, in order to alleviate these concerns.

Q. Would you be able to work extended hours as necessary to perform the job?

A. I'm accustomed to working long hours during the week. I usually work until at least six-thirty, because I get a lot done after the business office closes at five. I can make arrangements to be available on weekends, if necessary, though I do prefer to have at least twenty four hours' notice.

Your response should match closely the position you're applying for and should reflect a realistic understanding of the work and time required. Ask about seasonality of work, if you're unsure, and show a willingness to work occasional extended hours.

Q. Sell me this stapler.

A. This is a professional-quality stapler, designed to be functional as well as attractive. It will help you reduce clutter on your desk by enabling you to fasten pages together. And since papers relating to the same subject will now be attached, you'll be more efficient and will save time searching for papers. Finally, its sleek shape and black color are coordinated to match the rest of your office furniture.

With this kind of question the interviewer will want to determine how quickly you think on your feet, as well as your ability to communicate effectively and succinctly. Be prepared to give a thirty-second speech on the benefits and advantages of virtually any common office object, from a paper clip to a telephone, particularly if you're interviewing for a sales position.

Q. How do you feel when things go wrong with a project? How do you handle it?

A. Well, of course I would prefer that my projects run smoothly at all times. However, the very nature of the biotechnology industry means that many changes can and probably will happen to any plan at any time. I try to realize this from the outset and cross each bridge when I come to it. Often I try to have alternate plans ready to go in case of such an event. But sometimes you can't prepare for a problem until it's right there in front of you. Basically I just take it in stride.

This question is tricky. Yet the candidate understands this and has convinced the recruiter that he or she can deal with project setbacks without losing professional composure. The recruiter probably will not ask directly, "Can you work under pressure?"

This is what he or she is after. Responding "I crack under the pressure" to this question is not the way to go.

Q. Prove to me that your interest is sincere.

A. I know that a lot of people want to get into television because of the money or because they just want to be on camera. But to me, communicating well is an art, and the television industry is the ultimate test of how well one communicates. Working in television isn't like working for a newspaper, where if a reader misses a fact, he or she can just go back and reread it. A television news story can go by in a flash, and the challenge is to make sure the audience understands it, learns from it, and, in a broader sense, can use the information to better their lives or their situations. It's the way television can evoke action that's always made me want to be a part of the industry.

I'm particularly interested in this station because I like your focus on the community. Though the on-air products have great nineties look, it's to your credit that the station seems to remain focused on the tradition of local news and what matters to its audience. The special reports that emphasize town politics, which go on location each week to a different town for a live shot, that explain the big issues facing a community, make the viewer feel that the station is a part of the community. In my opinion this is a great way to maintain a loyal audience.

Being unprepared to answer this question can eliminate you from further consideration. On the other hand, if you're able to demonstrate a strong interest in the company and in the position, you'll have an advantage over the competition.

Q. Tell me about you.

A. I'm a production assistant with a B.A. in communications and three years of solid broadcasting and public-relations experience. I have extensive experience developing and researching topics, pre interviewing guests, and producing on-location video tapings. I have a tremendous amount of energy and love to be challenged. I'm constantly trying to take on additional responsibilities and learn new things.

I've been watching your station for some time now, and I've been impressed with your innovative approach and your fast growth. I'd like to be a part of that winning team.

This is a perfect opportunity to sell your qualifications to the interviewer. Using the sixty-second pitch you developed in chapter 1 as a guideline, briefly describe your experience, skills, accomplishments, goals, and personal qualities. Explain your interest in the company you're interviewing with and how you plan on making a contribution there. If you're a recent college graduate, be sure to discuss your educational qualifications as well, emphasizing the specific classes you took that are relevant to the position.

Q. What is your biggest weakness?

A. I admit to being a bit of a perfectionist. I take a great deal of pride in my work and am committed to producing the highest-quality work I can. Sometimes if I'm not careful, though, I can go a bit overboard. I've learned that it's not always possible or even practical to try to perfect your work—sometimes you have to decide what's important and ignore the rest in order to be productive. It's a question of trade-offs. I also pay a lot of attention to pacing my work, so that I don't get too caught up in perfecting every last detail.

This is a great example of what's known as a negative question. Negative questions are a favourite among interviewers, because they're effective for uncovering problems or weaknesses. The key to answering negative questions is to give them a positive spin. For this particular question your best bet is to admit to a weakness that isn't catastrophic, inconsistent, or currently disruptive to your chosen professional field, and to emphasize how you've overcome or minimized the problem. Whatever you do, don't answer this question with a copout like "I can't think of any," or even worse, "I don't really have any major weaknesses." This kind of response is likely to eliminate you from contention.

Q. You have seven minutes to convince me why you're the best candidate for this position.

Go.

Instead of following a traditional question-and-answer format for a job interview, some recruiters have been known to ask no more than this one question. Only the most prepared candidates will survive this type of interview. If you run into this question, your best bet is to discuss the various sales themes you developed, emphasizing one or two of your strongest qualifications for the position.

Q. How would you respond to a defaulted form Z-65 counter derivative renewal request if your manager ordered you to do so, and if the policy under which the executive board resolves such issues were currently under review?

Sometimes recruiters ask seemingly impossible questions just to see how you'll respond. It's not so much that they want to see you squirm in your seat as that they want to judge how you might respond to pressure or tension on the job. No matter how you may feel at the time, being subjected to a ridiculous question like this one is probably a very good sign. If you're asked a tough question that you simply can't answer, think about it for a few seconds. Then, with a confident smile and without apology, simply say something like "I don't know, but if you hire me, I'll sure find out for you."

Special Situations

Interviewing can be even more stressful when you find your self in what we call a special situation. Perhaps you lack paid job experience, have been out of the workplace to raise children, are concerned about possible discrimination because of age or disability, or are trying to enter a field in which you have no practical experience. Not to worry! The key to improving your chances in an interview is to emphasize your strengths. Focus on your marketable skills (whether they were acquired in the workplace or elsewhere), and highlight impressive achievements, relevant education and training, and/or related interests. And, of course, you should take care to downplay or eliminate any information that may be construed as a weakness.

For example, if you are a "displaced homemaker" (a homemaker entering the job market for the first time), you can highlight the special skills you've acquired over the years while down playing your lack of paid job experience.

Questions for Students and Recent Graduates

Whether you're graduating from high school or college, those of you with little or no work history face the same dilemma: it's tough to get a job without experience, and it seems impossible to gain experience without getting hired.

But, as you'll see, there are ways to get around this problem by emphasizing your strengths and educational achievements.

Q. Why weren't your grades better?

A. School was a wonderful experience for me. I really enjoyed learning new ideas, I studied consistently, and I was attentive in class. But I never believed in cramming before the night of an exam just to get a higher grade or staying up all night to finish a term paper. I really believe I taught just as much as many students who went for the grades.

It's likely that if you've made it to the interview stage, you fulfill the basic criteria for the position, including the education requirements. The recruiter is probably trying to judge here how well the candidate handles adversity. It's important not to get defensive or to place blame. Instead, try to put a positive spin on the question—for example, by concentrating on what you learned and the extra effort you put in, rather than on the grades you received.

Q. Why did you decide to major in history?

A. It was a difficult choice because I was also attracted to government, international relations, and economics.

But the study of history allowed me to combine all three, especially by focusing on economic history.

What's more, I found several of the professors in the department to be exceptionally knowledgeable and stimulating.

Show that you have solid, logical reasons for choosing your major. If you can't defend your choice of major, the interviewer will wonder how much thought you've put into choosing a career. You should also be sure that your reasons for choosing your major are compatible with your career choice. For instance, don't say you were English major because you love literature and writing if you're applying for a position as a banker.

Q. Was there a course that you found particularly challenging?

A. Initially I was completely overwhelmed by the introductory chemistry course that I took last year. No matter how hard I studied, I seemed to be getting nowhere. I failed the first three quizzes. So I tried a new approach. Instead of just studying by myself, I asked a friend whose chemistry major to help me with my studies. I also began seeking help from the professor after class. And I found that more time spent in the lab was critical. I ended up with a B-plus in the course and thought I achieved a solid understanding of the material. More than that, I learned that tackling a new field of study sometimes requires a new approach, not just hard work, and that the help of others can be crucial!

The interviewer will want to see how well you respond to difficult situations. Demonstrate that you won't fold in the face of difficulty, and that you're willing to put in the extra effort to meet a challenge.

Q. Why didn't you participate more in extracurricular activities?

A. I wanted to give ets much effort as possible to my studies. I came from a high school in a very small town, where I received a lot of As, but this didn't prepare me very well for college. So I studied very hard.

I have, however, found time to explore the city and make new friends, and I do socialize informally on weekends.

The interviewer may be worried that if you don't have many outside interests, you may eventually suffer from burnout. Employers like candidates who are well rounded and have interests outside of work. If you didn't participate in for mal extracurricular activities in college, you still may want to talk about some of your interests, such as reading or exercising, that you participated in on a more informal level. For instance, you may have a passion for running even if you weren't on the college track team.

Questions for Career Changers

For those of you who've devoted your careers exclusively to one profession or industry, work experience really isn't an issue. You have lots of experience—but none of it relates to your current job objective. No problem! Instead of emphasizing your job history, you'll just have to emphasize the skills you've acquired that apply to the job you're seeking. For example, let's say your career has been in real estate and, in your spare time, you like to run in marathons. Recently you heard about an opening in the sales-and-marketing department at an athletic-shoe manufacturer. What you need to do is emphasize the skills you have that the employer is looking for. Not only do you have strong sales experience, you're familiar with the needs of the company's market, and that's a powerful combination!

Q. Why do you want to leave your current position?

A. I've learned quite a bit about the plastics industry in my current position and am very glad to have had the opportunities I've had at Fiske, Inc. However, I've found that my interests really lie in research and development, which Fiske has recently decided to phase out over the next two years. And that's why I'm so interested in this organization, because, as I understand, Randy Corporation places a great deal of emphasis on R&D, and is also a highly respected

leader in the industry.

The interviewer's foremost concern with career changers will always be why they want to switch careers. Show the interviewer that your decision has been based on careful consideration. Explain why you decided upon this particular position, as well as how the position will allow you to further your natural skills and interests.

Q. Why would you want to leave an established career at an employment agency for an essentially entry-level position in marketing?

A. I've enjoyed my work at the agency and have gained many valuable skills from it At the same time, however, I feel as if I've stopped growing. I'm no longer challenged by my work. I've thought about this for a long time, and I'm confident that it's time for a change.

As for my interest in marketing, last year my teenage children and some of the other neighbourhood kids decided to design and sell T-shirts to benefit a local family who'd lost their home to afire. I pitched in by designing and distributing posters, placing advertisements in local newspapers, and selling shirts outside grocery stores and shopping malls. At first I really didn't give the project a lot of thought, but when I saw the fruits of my labour, I began to get very excited about it. I learned that you can have a great product and a great cause, but if nobody knows about it, you're dead in the water. I finally felt as if I was making a difference—and I was good at it, too. Since then I've taken two introductory marketing courses and am planning to enroll in a part-time degree program this fall.

Furthermore, I'll be able to use many of the skills and abilities I've gained at the employment agency in the marketing field. After all, working for an employment agency is marketing—marketing the agency to corporate clients and job seekers, and marketing job seekers to corporate clients.

The interviewer is trying to determine two things: the candidate's motivation for choosing a new career, and the likelihood that the candidate will be comfortable in a position where he or she will probably have less power and responsibility than in previous jobs. To dispel the interviewer's fears, discuss your reasons for switching careers, and be sure to show that you have a solid understanding of the position and the industry in general. Many candidates expect to start their new careers in a job comparable to the one they held previously. But the truth is that most career changers must start in lower—if not entry-level—positions in their new company to gain basic experience and knowledge of the field.

Questions for Candidates Re-entering the Job Market

There's no doubt about it, if you've been out of the work force for a while, you're facing some troubling issues. You may be feeling anxious, wondering if you've still got what it takes to make it out there. The key element for you is to make sure all of your skills are up-to-date. If they aren't, you should consider retraining, which might mean learning a new computer program or taking a class at the local college. If your skills are current, you have not to worry. What you'll need to emphasize is your previous job experience and skills, ways you've kept up-to-date during your leave, and the skills you've learned at home that can be transferred to the work place.

Q. Your resume doesn't list any job experience in the past few years. Why not?

A. J took five years off to raise my son, Jason, who's now in kindergarten. It was a difficult decision for me, but at the time, I decided I wouldn't be able to commit myself 100 percent to my career with such tremendous responsibilities at home. And I didn't think it would be fair to my employer to give any less than my complete and total commitment. I believe it was the right decision for me at the time, but now I feel refreshed and ready to devote myself full-time to my career.

Whatever the reason for your hiatus, be honest. Discuss the decisions behind your absence, whether they were to stay home and raise a family or to recuperate from a debilitating injury. Tell the interviewer why you're now ready to return to work. Most important, emphasize your eagerness to resume your career.

Q. I see you've been out of work for a while. What difficulties have you had in finding a job that's compatible with your interests?

A. It's true that I've been out of my field for the last four years, but I've had a number of tempting offers to jump back in. However, I thought it was important to stay home with my new baby and also continue a part-time family business, which I ran out of our home while my husband was completing law school.

Now that that's behind us, I'm ready to return to my career in the entertainment industry.

The real question behind the interviewer's curiosity here is why someone else hasn't taken this candidate off the market.

Why isn't the candidate in greater demand? Is he or she being too unrealistic or perhaps going after random positions? Is there something in the job seeker's past that others have discovered? You'll need to alleviate such concerns by frankly discussing your situation. Be sure to emphasize how you've remained involved in your career during your sabbatical, as well as your eagerness to rejoin the workforce.

Q. Your resume indicates that you've been working for the past two years as a part-time clerk at Reliable Insurance Brokers. How will this experience help you in your banking career?

A. Reliable was in the process of computerizing its files, and I was hired primarily to check the computerized files for accuracy vis-a-vis the manual files. I recorded premium payments, prepared bank deposits, and sorted payables. Not only did this work help me keep my accounting skills current, I also learned valuable computer skills that will certainly help me become even more efficient and productive in my next position in banking.

The interviewer may be concerned here that the candidate is simply applying for any available job, rather than for a specific position in a specific field. Explain how your experience relates to the position you're applying for, and discuss any skills you've gained that are transferable to the position and company.

Illegal Interview Questions

Illegal interview questions probe into your private life or personal background. Federal law forbids employers from discriminating against any person on the basis of sex, age, race, national origin, or religion. For instance, an interviewer may not ask you about your age or your date of birth. However, she or he may ask you if you're over eighteen years of age.

If you're asked an illegal question at a job interview, keep in mind that many employers simply don't know what's legal and illegal. One strategy is to try to discover the concerns behind the question and then address them. For instance, if the employer asks you about your plans to have children, he or she may be concerned that you won't be able to fulfil the travel requirements of the position. You bet. But it's to your advantage to try to alleviate those concerns.

TV to get to the heart of the issue behind the question by saying something likes "I'm not quite sure I understand what you're getting at. Would you please explain to me how this issue is relevant to the position?" Once the interviewer's real concerns are on the table, you can allay those concerns by saying something like "I'm very interested in developing my career. Travel is definitely not a problem for me—in fact, I enjoy it tremendously. Now, let me direct your attention to my experience and expertise in . . ."

Alternatively, you may choose to answer the question or to gracefully point out that the question is illegal and decline to respond. Avoid reacting in a hostile fashion—remember that you can always decide later to decline a job offer.

Any of the following responses are acceptable ways to handle these tricky situations without blowing your chances for a job offer. Choose the response that's most comfortable for you.

Q. What religion do you practice?

Answer 1: I make it a point not to mix my personal beliefs with my work, if that's what you mean. I assure you that I value my career too much for that.

Answer 2: I'm not quite sure I understand what you're getting at. Would you please explain to me how this issue is relevant to the position?

Answer 3: That question makes me uncomfortable. I'd really rather not answer it.

Q. How old are you?

Answer 1: I'm in my fifties and have over thirty years of experience in this industry. My area of expertise is in.

Answer 2: I'm too young to retire, but I'm old enough to know better than to answer a question like that.

Answer 3: I'm not quite sure I understand what you're getting at. Would you please explain to me how this issue is relevant to the position?

Answer 4: That question makes me uncomfortable. I'd really rather not answer it.

Q. Are you married?

Answer l: No.

Answer 2: Yes, I am. But I keep my family life separate from my work life so that I can put all my effort into my job. I'm flexible when it comes to travel and late hours, as my references can confirm.

Answer 3: I'm not quite sure I understand what you're getting at. Would you please explain to me how this issue is relevant to the position?

Answer 4: That question makes me uncomfortable. I'd really rather not answer it.

Q. Do you have children?

Answer 1: No.

Answer 2: Yes, I do. But I keep my family life separate from my work life so that I can put all my effort into my job. I'm flexible when it comes to travel and late hours, as my references can confirm.

Answer 3: I'm not quite sure I understand what you're getting at. Would you please explain to me how this issue is relevant to the position?

Answer 4: That question makes me uncomfortable. I'd really rather not answer it.

Q. Do you plan to have children?

Answer 1: No.

Answer 2: It's certainly a consideration, but if I do, it won't be for some time. I want to do the best job I can for this company and have no plans to leave just as I begin to make meaningful contributions.

Answer 3: J can't answer that right now. But if I ever do decide to have children, I wouldn't let it detract from my work. Becoming a parent is important, but my career is certainly very important to me, too. I plan on putting all of my efforts into this job and this company.

Answer 4: I'm not quite sure I understand what you're getting at. Would you please explain to me how this issue is relevant to the position?

Answer 5: That question makes me uncomfortable. I'd really rather not answer it.

Q. What environments allow you to be especially effective?

A. Although I can work effectively in most environments, I prefer environments where people are their own bosses, within reason. I like to have a goal but be able to draw my own map to get there. To accomplish goals, I rely on asking questions and finding people receptive, so cooperation and access are important to me in a work group. Emphasize your flexibility and your ability to work in many different types of environments. Your answer should not consist of a laundry list of requirements (private office, few interruptions, and so on) or the interviewer may conclude that you will be difficult to satisfy

Q. Describe an environment that is ineffective for you.

A. I don't do terribly well when someone has an exact idea of how one of my goals should be accomplished.

That doesn't allow me any latitude to make adjustments to suit my own style. I do well when I can draw my own map.

This is the negative side of "What environments allow you to be especially effective?" Focus on environments you prefer or that increase your effectiveness.

Q. What situations excite and motivate you?

A. I really enjoy working on any re-engineering project where a true improvement results—for example, the JIT project in which we saved more than ten thousand dollars per month in inventory costs.

The interviewer wants a clearer perspective as to what kind of work inspires you. There is no one right answer to this question, but your answer should be at least somewhat compatible with the position you're applying for. For example, you should not say that highly creative work motivates you if you're applying for a position that involves somewhat monotonous, repetitive work, such as data entry or assembly-line work.

Q. How would your last employer describe your work habits and ethics?

A. Let I put it this way: I received an MVP award from my division for the extra efforts I put into one of our customer relationships. The customer had threatened to pull the account, so I stepped in and debugged the system, even though it required me to work through a holiday weekend.

Do you think your current or last employer would hire you again? Are you reliable, thorough, and dependable? Give examples of your reliability, dedication, and corporate loyalty

Q. How do you feel your company treats its employees?

A. In recent years, management has really been dedicated to having a satisfied workforce. Their efforts, however, often rekindle past upheavals, when employees made sacrifices for the company and received little in return.

In human resources we spend a lot of money trying to break down the walls between exempt and non-exempt employees. If "the company" is management, I would have to say management is making a conscious effort to mend fences and to do right by our employees.

The interviewer wants to see if you can walk the fine line between loyalty to management and concern for the employees. Although there's no right answer to this question, you should try to avoid bias and to comment as objectively as possible on your company's attitude and approach toward employees. Be prepared to give examples that reflect your company's view toward its employees.

Q. Did your customers or clients enjoy working with you?

A. My client base changed very little, except that billings increased, so I think that's evidence the clients were satisfied enough to stay with me for more than three years. That's particularly unusual in the ad-agency business, too. They simply knew they could count on me to treat their business as if it were my own.

How would the company's customers or clients react to you? Can you give specific feedback from a client? How many of your clients were repeat customers? Why do you believe you kept their business?

Q. How will you complement this department?

A. I enjoy an environment in which people bounce ideas off each other and have the flexibility to ask for help when they need it. I'm usually a great trouble shooter for PC problems in my office, and I'm often going to ask for help proofreading important memos. I believe in give-and-take.

Describe how your personality and/or skills would help round out the department. What types of people enjoy working with you for hours at a time? How would the company's customers or clients react? Assure the interviewer that there will be no surprises about your work personality.

Q. Whom did you choose as your references, and why?

A. J selected a former boss, a peer, and a customer as references, to demonstrate that I'm a pretty well rounded person and get along with all the important work associates in my life.

The interviewer is looking for a logical mix of people without any obvious omissions. For example, a former salesperson would do well to include a former salesperson as a reference.

Describe what you'd expect each of your references to say. Include a diverse group—senior to junior, an associate from work, an old professor from college.

Q. Can we call all of your references?

A. I'd prefer that you call my current boss only after you've made me a firm offer of employment and I've had a chance to tell her myself that I'm changing jobs. Then, of course, I understand your need to verify that my application was accurate.

This is a question designed to protect you. If your current employer doesn't know you're looking for a new job, you can request that the interviewer contact your current employer only after you've accepted a position and given your notice to your current employer.

Q. Tell me what you learned from a recent book.

A. I enjoy reading biographies, especially of people who lived in a different era. I recently read Churchill's biography, which taught mea lot about the value of leadership and good PR under times of stress.

The interviewer wants to know if the candidate has interests in common with others at the company. Do you use your spare time as a productive, yet relaxing, way to learn new things? What are you naturally inquisitive about?

Q. Tell me about a work group you really enjoyed.

A. My group in our new-product-launch department really meshed. When one of us was approaching the final day before a launch, we all rolled up our sleeves and helped put press packets together or whatever else was the last item to be shipped to the sales force.

Although it was an administrative task, it had to be done, and it wets a good time for us all to speculate on the success of the product and any major concerns.

This question is a combination of "Describe your working relationship with your colleagues," and "Did your customers or clients enjoy working with you?" Demonstrate your ability to work well with others and to establish solid, ongoing working relationships.

Q. Describe a time when you had to assist a co-worker.

A. I once helped an associate understand survey methodology in order to write a report. He had never taken a research course and didn't know how to structure questions.

Demonstrate a willingness to pitch in. Discuss a time when your objective advice or special expertise produced a positive outcome for a co-worker and for the department.

Q. Are you most productive working alone or in a group?

A. I need some private time for planning, but otherwise I like the activity and noise of people around me and the ability to share ideas. I think most writers need reinforcement, because we all get writer's block occasionally.

The interviewer is looking for someone who can work in an environment without the environment disrupting the can did ate's preferred way of getting work done. Be honest but communicate that you're a flexible and reasonably adaptable employee.

Q. Tell me about a situation in which it was difficult to remain objective.

A. I'd researched a new on-line source for our library, and my manager decided to pull funding at the last minute. It was frustrating for me because I'd gotten excited about the product, liked the vendor, and had even told some people to count on having the resource.

But I understand the need to revise budgets, and the matter was out of my control at the time.

The obvious example here is a time when you've worked long hours on a project only to have the project cancelled. Or perhaps you found that the project was less strategically sound than you'd hoped. Were you able to readjust your thinking and do what was best in the long run?

Q. Tell me about a project in which you were disappointed with your personal performance.

A. In my last job for a manufacturing company, I had to analyze all of the supplier bids and present recommendations to the vice president of logistics.

Because the supplier bids weren't in a uniform format, my analysis often consisted of comparing dissimilar items. This caused some confusion in my final report, and by the time Yd reworked it and presented it to the vice president, we'd lost the critical time we needed to improve our approval process for these bids. In hindsight I should have taken a simpler approach to the problem and not tried to make it so complex or all inclusive. Ever since, I've paid more attention to making recommendations in a timely manner.

Describe roadblocks and what you've done to try to get around them. How have your skills come into play? In hind sight, what could you have done differently? What lessons have you learned?

Q. What would you do if I told you that I thought you were giving a very poor interview today?

A. Well, the first thing I'd do is ask you if there were any specific part of the interview that you thought I might have mishandled. After that I'd think back and try to remember if there had been any faulty communication on my part. Then I'd try to review possible problems I had understanding your questions, and I'd ask for clarification if I needed it. Finally, if we had time, I'd try to respond mournfully and appropriately to the problem areas you identified for me.

Interviewers like to ask stress questions like these to see how well you hold up under pressure. Your best bet is to stay calm and relaxed; don't allow your confidence to be shaken.

Q. Tell me about your most difficult work or personal experience.

A. One time my co-worker went through rehab for six months after a wreck, and I picked up a lot of additional work to help him out. I know he would've done the same for me, and it's important for me to have that kind of trust among the members of my workgroup.

The interviewer will want to know how you hold up under pressure. Describe a situation, either personal or professional, that involved a great deal of conflict and challenge and placed you under an unusual amount of stress. What, specifically, were the problems, and what did you do to resolve them?

Q. If this were your first annual review with our company, what would I be telling you right now?

A: You'd be thanking me for a job well done and would be explaining how you look forward to continuing to see good work from me. Furthermore, I would anticipate your explaining how you really appreciated my putting in extra time on some key projects and how my creative thinking helped come up with some innovative solutions to existing problems.

For this question you obviously want to present a positive impression. "I wish you would show up on time more," is definitely not a good answer. Remember to focus on one or two of your key strengths based on the personal themes you've developed.

Q. Give an example of a time when you were asked to accomplish a task but weren't given enough information. How did you resolve this problem?

A. At my last internship, my supervisor, an account executive, asked me to assemble five hundred press kits for a mailing. I wasn't sure in what order the pages and press releases should go, but my supervisor had already left for a client meeting. Afraid of putting the information together in the wrong order, I managed to track down her cell-phone number and called her in her car. She explained the order of the materials over the phone, and in the end I managed to prevent a mistake that would have cost hours of work and a delay in the mailing—not to mention a few headaches.

Although this example may seem trivial, the candidate demonstrates maturity and an ability to approach work conceptually. The interviewer will want to know that you understand that just getting the job done isn't enough. Your response should show resourcefulness and initiative.

Q. Describe a time when you failed to resolve a conflict.

A. I wasn't able to keep a good employee once who'd been in our manufacturing facility for ten years. His job description was rewritten to require computer skills. I offered to send him to night classes, but he refused the help. I had no option but to replace him. In retrospect, if I'd encouraged him and other employees to acquire new training periodically, he might not have been overwhelmed by the time his position was reworked.

Now I'm vigilant about encouraging my group to attend seminars and courses to enhance their job skills and to avoid becoming outdated.

The ideal solution here is to discuss a conflict that wasn't yours to solve in the first place. If you must discuss a personal conflict, focus on the positive steps you'd take if you could go back and do it over again. What have you learned as a result of this experience?

Q. How have you handled criticism of your work?

A. The first time I had a complaint from a client, I found it difficult to keep the complaint separate from my professional service of the account The client was upset about the downtime on ATM machines. I learned that showing empathy usually calms an unpleasant situation; I also learned that no client is going to be happy with everything, even if that client's overall experience is positive.

The interviewer is looking for an indication of the candidate's accountability and professional character. Describe a specific project or work habit that caused you a problem until you faced up to it and overcame it. Alternatively, you might describe a time you responded objectively and professionally to particularly harsh or unreasonable criticism of your work.

Q. What aspects of your work are most often criticized?

A: I remember in my first job as marketing assistant I spent endless hours analyzing a particular problem. I came up with a revised marketing plan that was extremely well received. Unfortunately, when it came time to present the plan to top management, I hadn't prepared the fine points of the presentation—overheads and slides—and the proposal were turned down. I'd failed to make clear the savings that would result from the plan. I spent the next two weeks working on my presentation, and on my second try management approved it, and my recommendations were carried out to everyone's satisfaction.

This question is similar to the question on weaknesses. Try to give an example from an early job. Discuss what you did to overcome the situation and to improve your work. You could also discuss how the failure has inspired you to pay more careful attention to detail in all your work.

Q. Tell me about the last time you put your foot in your mouth.

A: I told my friend Lisa that I'd no longer be attending yearbook-club meetings because I thought the editor was a complete idiot. I later found out that the editor was her cousin. As soon as I found out, I apologized and asked her why she didn't say anything when I made that foolish comment. Luckily, she and I are still friends today. Everyone makes mistakes, and it's important for you to be cognizant of yours. The interviewer will want to find out if you have a sense of right and wrong, and what steps you're willing to take to provide restitution for your mistakes.

Leaving someone with a bad impression of you, your company, or your client can be very detrimental to your firm.

Q. What might your current boss want to change about your work habits?

A. I'm a morning person and she's a night owl. I like to come into the office at least an hour early, usually by seven, to get a jump start on my work. My boss likes to come in after nine and work late into the evening.

So I think if she could change one thing about me, she'd probably make me into a night owl, too, so that I'd be available during many of the same hours she likes to work.

The interviewer will want to know how you'll fit in with your future boss and co-workers, and will also want to feel confident that he or she has uncovered any surprises about your corporate style. One good way to answer this question is to point out minor differences of preference. Alternatively, you might describe a weakness that you and your boss have worked on and improved.

Q. Tell me about two or three aspects of your last job you'd never want to repeat.

A; I'm glad that I have experience in credit collections because it's enabled me to make better risk assessments. I really didn't enjoy the work, though, and it isn't something I want to do again.

In a constructive way, describe two or three things you've done that you didn't especially enjoy or that didn't play upon your strengths. Then describe your strengths and their relevance to the job you're applying for.

Q. Tell me about a situation that frustrated you at work.

A. J was frustrated once when one of my clients, who'd insisted on a high growth stock, called in a panic because the stock price had dropped more than twenty points in one day I had a hard time convincing him to ride it out rather than cut his losses. This happened despite my attempts from the beginning to explain the short-term volatility of that stock.

This is another question designed to probe the candidate's professional personality. The interviewer will want reassurance that you are able to hold up under pressure. Describe how you've remained diplomatic, objective, or professional in a difficult situation.

Q. Tell me about one of your projects that failed.

A. I've always had the tendency to be a workaholic, and have the attitude that I can tackle anything and achieve good results. During the hurricane of 1992, my insurance company was inundated with claims. I immediately thought I could handle all the claims in my area and jumped in with both feet to work eighteen-hour days. I quickly realized, though, that there was no way I could complete all of the claims on time, and I had to start to delegate some of the responsibility to my investigators. This experience showed me that no matter how efficient and competent you are, there are times when you must either delegate responsibility or ask for help.

Demonstrate the ability here to be humble and to learn from your mistakes. In hindsight, what could you have done differently? How has your leadership style changed because of the experience?

Q. Tell me about a time when your employer wasn't happy with your job performance.

A. That would be during my first week on the job as a paralegal. I gave her two letters that had typos in them. Frankly, I'd simply been a little sloppy—but that's the only example that comes to mind. Ms. Heilman did tell me regularly that she was very happy with my work.

Again, be sure to discuss a relatively minor incident here.

Also, show a willingness to accept responsibility for the problem—don't blame others or make excuses. Simply describe what happened and how you successfully resolved the situation.

Q. Have you ever been passed up for a promotion that you felt you deserved?

A. A couple of times in my early career I thought that I was unfairly passed up for a promotion. However, in retrospect I now realize that in all likelihood I wasn't ready to perform in those jobs—and, in fact, the additional training experience I gained remaining where I was proved invaluable in the last few years, as I've made significant progress moving up the corporate ladder. I've also learned to appreciate that being ready for a promotion doesn't necessarily mean it'll happen. There are many external factors that influence the nature and timing of promotions, aside from a person's performance and capabilities.

The interviewer wants to gauge the candidate's self-confidence, as well as his or her objectivity about personal or professional limitations. Give evidence here that you have enough patience to learn what's important before you get bored or frustrated. After you've mastered your own job, would you stay motivated long enough to be productive?

Q. Have you ever been fired?

A. During one of my summer internships while in college, I worked for a software consulting company. Midway through the summer a new president was appointed because of some financial difficulties, and he requested the resignation of my entire group. I wets swept out with everyone else, even though my work performance had never been criticized.

If you've never been fired, of course, this is a simple question to answer. But if you have been fired, you'll need to be prepared to discuss the situation in detail and possibly answer a series of very specific follow-up questions. If the termination was a result of a situation beyond your control, such as corporate downsizing, most interviewers will be very understanding. But if you were fired due to poor performance or some other problem, you'll need to admit your fault and convince the interviewer that you've corrected the problem.

Although this may be a difficult question to answer, you should be completely honest. If you aren't, and the recruiter finds out as much from your references, you may be subject to immediate dismissal, or your job offer may be revoked.

Q. Why have you changed jobs so frequently?

A. My frequent job changes over the last five years have been due to the rapid changes in my profession. My jobs have been based on government contracts, and over the last several years congressional appropriations have been up and down, causing some companies' contracts to be cancelled, while other companies land huge, unexpected contracts. This volatility creates some good opportunities, but it also creates a lot of uncertainty. Because your business is based mostly on consumer products, and not on government products, I welcome the opportunity to work in an environment where the business cycle is more stable and predictable.

Be candid here. Personal growth, a larger budget, or other career-enhancing experiences are all valid reasons for moving on. Convince the interviewer that you're interested in his or her company for the long haul.

Q. Why did you stay in your last job so long?

A. I was in my last job over seven years. During that time, I completed an advanced technical degree and also had two six-month assignments in which I was loaned out to different departments. As a result, I acquired some additional skills that normally aren't associated with that particular job. Therefore, I think I've made good progress and am ready to accept the next challenge.

The interviewer may be curious about your interest in personal improvement, tackling new assignments, and so on. He or she may also be concerned about whether you have a tendency to get too comfortable with the status quo.

Demonstrate how you've developed job responsibilities in meaningful new ways.

Q. Tell me about a problem you've had getting along with a work associate.

A. I'm pretty easygoing and tend to get along with most people. But I remember one time when we brought in a new associate who was very bossy—to the point where he offended one of our interns with his attitude. I actually pulled him aside and told him that I found it more productive to ask people for help than to give orders. Unfortunately, my advice didn't seem to help much, but we were more careful when we hired new staff after that.

Avoid discussing a personality clash; focus instead on a difference in work ethic between you and an associate, or something else with which the interviewer is likely to empathize.

For example, you might describe someone whose standards of excellence were perhaps less stringent than yours.

Q. Tell me about your least-favourite manager or professor.

A. Well, I've been pretty fortunate as far as managers go, and I didn't have any problems with my professors. In my first job out of college I worked with a manager who was pretty inaccessible. If you walked into his office to ask a question, you got the sense that you were bothering him, so we just learned to get help from each other instead. I wouldn't say he was my least-favourite manager, because he was a good manager in a lot of ways, but I would have preferred that he'd made himself more available to us and given us more direction.

Answering this question will be a little bit like walking across a loaded minefield, so beware! Keep in mind that the interviewer doesn't want to learn about your former supervisors; he or she does want to learn about the way you speak about them. Though the interviewer may bait you to make a negative statement about your former employer, doing so can create a host of problems. Even if your claim is completely true and entirely justified, the recruiter may conclude either that you don't get along well with people or that you shift blame to others. The best way around this dilemma is to choose an example that's not too negative, touch upon it briefly, then focus the rest of your answer on what you learned from the experience.

Q. Who's the toughest employer you've ever had, and why?

A. That would be Ms. Henson at Franklin Associates.

She'd push people to their limits when things got busy, and she wets a stickler for detail. But she was always fair, and she rewarded good, hard work. I'd call her a tough boss, but a good boss

Again, you should avoid making negative statements about your previous employers, at all costs. Turn the question around with a positive, upbeat response, as this candidate does.

Q. Have you ever had to work with a manager who was unfair to you, or who was just plain hard to get along with?

A. Actually, I've never run into that. Of course, my current boss has to work under time constraints—just like everyone else—and she sometimes has to phrase things succinctly if our department is going to meet its goals. But I've never considered that unfair or hard to handle. It's just part of the job. My supervisors and I have always gotten along quite well.

Never, under any circumstances, criticize a current or former employer; no matter how many times the interviewer gives you the opportunity to do so. What the interviewer is trying to find out here is not whether the candidate has worked for difficult people, but if he or she is willing to bad-mouth them.

CHAPTER 8

Win the Deal

You've made it through the toughest part—but now what? First, breathe a sigh of relief! Then, as soon as you've left the interview site, write down your thoughts about the interview while they're still fresh in your mind. Ask yourself these key questions:

- What does the position entail?
- What do you like and dislike about the position and the company?
- Did you make any mistakes or have trouble answering any of the questions?
- Did you feel you were well prepared?
- If not, what could you do to improve your performance in the future?

Carefully consider all of these questions; if you find that your performance was lacking, work to improve it.

Be sure to record the name and title of the person you inter viewed with, as well as the names and titles of anyone else you may have met. Ideally, you'll have collected their business cards. Don't forget to write down what the next agreed-upon step will be. Will the recruiter contact you? How soon?

Writing Your Follow-Up Letter

It's fair to say that follow-up letters won't necessarily help you secure the job, but not sending one will most certainly hurt your chances. You should write a follow-up letter immediately after each interview you have, ideally within twenty four hours. The letter should be brief (no more than a page) and personalized. In your letter, you should be sure to:

- Express your appreciation for the opportunity to interview with the recruiter.
- Express your continued enthusiasm about the position and the company.
- Recap your strengths, being careful to relate them to the requirements of the job and the company.
- Request to meet again.

The following is an example of a good follow-up letter:

Sample Follow-Up Letter

178 N. Green Park
New Delhi, India -110011
(312)555-5555
(312)555-5050
October 12, 2016

Pat Cummings
Personnel Manager
Any Corporation
1140 Park Avenue,
Kolkata, West Bengal-700001

Dear Ms.Payal:

It was a pleasure meeting with you yesterday regarding the research-assistant position. I enjoyed learning more about the opportunity and about Any Corporation.

The position is exciting and seems to encompass a diversity of responsibilities. I believe that with my experience and skills, I'm qualified to make a valuable contribution to your organisation.

Should you require additional information, please don't hesitate to contact me at either telephone number listed above or at (312) 555-1212.

I look forward to hearing from you.

Sincerely,

Janak Singh

Allow the interviewer five to ten business days to contact you after receiving your letter. If you still haven't heard anything after that time, you should follow up with a phone call.

Express your continued interest in the firm and the position, and inquire as to whether or not a decision has been made or when you'll be notified.

In the meantime, it's important to keep your candidacy fresh in the interviewer's mind. Send work that intrigued the interviewer (for example, brochures or writing samples). If the conversation during the interview provided any possibilities for follow-up, such as reading an article or book, drop a note to the interviewer, mentioning how much you learned from the piece. Or if you discovered during the interview that you share common interests with the interviewer, such as sailing or rock climbing, consider sending the person a great article you just found on the topic. Not only will this ensure that you don't get lost in the shuffle, it will help you establish a sense of camaraderie with the interviewer. Though this technique won't guarantee you the position, it certainly can't hurt if it gets the interviewer in your corner!

Taking the Next Step

Don't be discouraged if you don't receive an immediate response from an employer—most companies interview many applicants before making a final decision. Take advantage of this time to contact other firms, and to schedule more inter views, so that if a rejection does come, you have other options open. Continuing to job-hunt and to interview will have been a good idea even if you end up receiving the job offer.

Ultimately, you may have a number of opportunities to choose from, and you'll be in a better position to negotiate terms.

If you place too much importance on a single interview, not only are you bound to be unduly disappointed if the offer doesn't come through, you'll be wasting valuable time and energy. So keep plugging away!

Handling Rejection

Rejection is inevitable, and it's bound to happen to you just as it happens to all other job hunters. The key is to be prepared for it and not to take it personally.

One way you can turn rejection around is by contacting each person who sends you a rejection letter. Thank your con tact for considering you for the position and request that he or she keep you in mind for future openings. If you feel comfortable, you may want to ask the person for suggestions to help you improve your chances of getting a job in that industry or for the names of people who might be looking for someone with your skills. You may want to say something like "What would you do in my situation? Who would you call?"

Two cautions are in order: First, don't ask employers to tell you why they didn't hire you. Not only will this place a recruiter in a very awkward position, you'll probably get a very negative reaction. Second, keep in mind that if you contact employers solely for impartial feedback, not everyone will be willing to talk to you.

A well-written thank-you note, mailed within one or two days of receiving notice of rejection, makes a positive statement. When Danny E was turned down for a position as a publicity director, he quickly wrote his interviewer a letter that expressed his disappointment at not being offered the job, but also his thanks for the company's consideration of his qualifications. The interviewer was so impressed by Danny's initiative; she provided him several contact names to assist in his continued search.

In your letter, emphasize an ongoing interest in being considered for future openings. Also, be very careful to use an upbeat tone. Although you may be disappointed, you don't want to put the employer on the defensive or imply that you don't respect his or her decision. Above all, don't give up! Stay positive and motivated, and learn from the process. Success could be right around the corner!

CHAPTER 9

The Final Negotiation

In today's tough economy, one of the most nerve-racking steps on the trail to a new job is near the end of the path: deciding whether or not to accept an offer. On the one hand, if you've been in the job market for some time, your instincts may scream, "I'll take it! I'll take it!" before the last syllables of the offer are out of the recruiter's mouth. On the other, you may also be worrying that the salary won't even cover the cost of all those stamps you've used to send out resumes and cover letters over the past few months.

Faced with these conflicting emotions, many job seekers can make unnecessary, costly mistakes during this final, vitally important stage. Far too many people sell themselves short without even exploring their options. Others have wildly unrealistic expectations of the level of compensation they should expect. Still others get so wrapped up in money questions they forget to consider other issues—a big mistake.

Important Factors to Consider

If you're going to consider a job offer seriously, be confident that this is a job you really want. If you're just graduating, is the job in the field you'd like to pursue? Are you willing to live and work in the area in question? Would you enjoy the work schedule? The way of life is?

Whether or not a job will help your career progress is ultimately a much more important question than what your starting salary will be. In some organizations, you may be given a lot of responsibility right away but then find your upward progress blocked. Make sure you know if there are opportunities for advancement. Ask about performance reviews: how often are they conducted?

Other information you should have in order to make a sound decision includes:

- Start date
- Job title and associated responsibilities
- Salary, overtime, and compensation
- Bonus structure
- Tuition reimbursement
- Vacation and parental-leave policy
- Life-, medical-, and dental-insurance coverage
- Pension plan
- Travel requirements

Ideally, these issues will have been covered during the course of the interview process or at the time the job offer is made. But if you're unsure of any of this information, don't assume that the specifics will be to your satisfaction. Contact the personnel representative or recruiter and confirm all important details.

Work Environment

Another important factor to consider is the kind of environment you'll be working in. Is the company's atmosphere comfortable, challenging, and exciting? Consider specifics, including office or workstation setting, privacy, proximity to other staff, amount of space, noise level, and lighting. How much interaction occurs between co-workers? Some organisations strongly encourage teamwork and dialogue among staff, whereas others prefer to emphasize individual accomplishment. Which approach works better for you? Remember: If you don't like the work environment before you accept the job, you probably won't like it as an employee.

Salary and Benefits

Money may seem like the biggest criterion in accepting a job, but it can often cloud the decision-making process. Don't accept a job that you're not enthusiastic about simply because the starting salary is a few thousand dollars higher than what you're currently making. It's probably more important to find a job that lets you do something you enjoy. Ask yourself whether the position presents a career path with upward movement and long-range income potential.

Benefits can make a big difference in your compensation package, so don't overlook them! Perhaps the most important benefit to consider is health insurance. With health-insurance costs skyrocketing, you should be sure to find out if the company covers these costs in full. If the company, like many others, pays only a percentage of these costs, make certain that you can afford to pay the difference out of your own pocket.

And what about life, dental, and disability insurance are? Does the company have a bonus structure or profit-sharing plan?

These things can contribute significantly to your salary. Is there a pension plan? How many vacation days or sick days will you get? You should consider all of these factors carefully.

If you plan to continue your education, it's important to find out if the organization will pay for your tuition and if the employer will give you time to attend classes. Some organisations offer tuition incentives but require so much overtime that it's very difficult to take advantage of the benefit.

Do Your Homework

Supplement the information that the organization provides by searching journals and newspapers for articles about the company and, if possible, by talking to current employees. Try to get objective comments—not for instance, information from someone who was recently fired by the company. Alumni of your college or university who hold similar positions or are employed by the same organization may be an excellent source of information.

Negotiating the Offer

The prospect of negotiating salary and benefits strikes fear into the hearts of many job seekers young and old. But handling the inevitable money questions doesn't have to be difficult.

And the more you think about them in advance, the easier they'll be for you to answer. Let's go through the process step by step.

First, the basics never try to negotiate salary or benefits until after you've gotten an offer. Try it, and you'll look as if you care more about money than about putting your skills to work for the company. Your goals at an interview are simple:

(1) prove to the recruiter that you're well-suited to the job as you understand it, and (2) make sure that you feel comfortable with the prospect of performing the job and working in the environment the company offers.

If you've been offered a position, congratulations! The hard part is over. If you feel uncomfortable about negotiating for a salary, relax. The tables are now turned in your favour. Think about it—you've already gotten what you want. Until you say yes to the offer, the burden is on the recruiter. He or she has put a lot of time and effort into finding the right candidate and has decided that you are that person. If you say no, the recruiter will have wasted a lot of energy and may have to go back to square one to find another candidate.

So don't worry about the recruiter's withdrawing his or her handshake and showing you the door if you dare to ask if the company's offer is flexible. The worst case might be that the employer tells you your salary is set by company policy and there's really no room to negotiate. But the recruiter may just as likely tell you he or she can't give you an immediate answer and will have to get back to you.

The most important thing to remember about salary negotiations are that most salaries are negotiable. That doesn't mean that you name a figure and the employer either matches it or doesn't. It means that you're ready to listen to what the recruiter has to offer, and give it consideration. To succeed in negotiation, both parties have to reach an agreement with which both are happy. If you somehow succeed at winning yourself a bigger pay check but antagonize your future boss in doing so, trouble lies ahead. If, on the other hand, you set realistic expectations and realize that you may not get everything you want, you'll probably do just fine.

Just how do you know how much you should expect? The answer is the same as in every other step of your job search:

Do your homework. Contact your professional association or read the trade journals for your industry. Call employment agencies to find out salaries of jobs listed with them; read the newspaper help-wanted ads. Alumni of your college or university in similar positions may also be an excellent source of information. Doing this research will give you an idea of the general salary level you can realistically expect.

Setting realistic expectations is especially important for the entry-level job seeker or recent graduate. If you don't have a lot of professional experience, you don't leave the recruiter with much hard evidence on which to base a decision. Instead, you're asking him or her to take a leap of faith based on potential that you've demonstrated in classes, internships, volunteer work, or extracurricular activities. Without a track record of professional experience, your arsenal is missing a powerful weapon. This is why entry-level salaries are often determined by the marketplace. That leaves you very little leverage with which to negotiate. Even so, that doesn't mean you can't give it a try.

On the other hand, if you have some experience under your belt and are looking for a midlevel or executive-level position, your negotiating power might be much greater. For a lucky few at the top of the heap, salary and benefit negotiations can be as complex and painstakingly slow as a bill passing through Congress. If you're like most people, you're not in that group. Whatever your level of experience, your task is to try to figure out just how high the employer is likely to go.

If, after listening politely to the specifics of the offer, you're left hoping for a higher salary, greater health coverage, or something else, it's okay to say so. Find out if the offer is firm. If it seems there may be some room to negotiate, make sure you have a specific figure in mind, because if the recruiter does have the freedom to barter, he or she will probably ask you point-blank to supply a figure that would satisfy you.

When you're asked that question, rule number one is as follows: Don't tip your hand by giving the interviewer a concrete number for which you're willing to settle. You don't want to take yourself out of the running by naming a figure that's absurdly optimistic, and you certainly don't want to risk naming a figure that's lower than what the employer is ready to offer. Instead of naming your price, say something like,

"Based on my experience and skills, and the demands of the position, I'd expect to earn an appropriate figure. Can you give me some idea what kind of range you have in mind?"

If you're pressed about salary requirements during an interview and you feel you must name a figure, give a salary range instead of your most recent salary. And don't forget to add in the value of your insurance, pension, or any other benefits you had.

Naming a salary range gives you a chance to hook on to a figure that's also in the range the company has in mind. In fact, many companies base their offers on sliding salary scales. Therefore, if you name a range of, say, twenty-five to thirty thousand dollars, it just may be that the company was considering a range of twenty-two to twenty-eight thousand dollars. In this case, you'll be more likely to receive an offer in the mid-to-upper end of your range. Of course, your experience and qualifications also play a part here. If you're just starting out and have little experience, the recruiter may be more likely to stick toward the lower end of the scale.

A few words about projecting the right attitude when discussing money—try not to reveal what you're thinking. Even if the salary offer seems barely above poverty level, it wouldn't be wise to inform the recruiter of that fact. Similarly, if the offer is much higher than you expected, doing cartwheels around the room probably wouldn't be appropriate, either. In all seriousness, though your appearance and demeanour are important throughout your career, they are especially important at the interview and offer stages. If you want to be a professional, start right away by acting like one.

Some final notes

The point of your job search isn't salary negotiation; it's finding a job that you'll be happy with, that you'll grow with, and that will allow you to be yourself. If your starting salary isn't the one you dreamed about, but the job presents the right opportunity, think about the possibility of commanding a higher salary once you've had a chance to make yourself invaluable to the organization.

On the other hand, if the salary or benefits fall far short of your realistic expectations, despite all your efforts to negotiate, nothing says you have to take the job. Don't make the mistake of accepting a position with which you're fundamentally unhappy. Trust your instincts—if you're dissatisfied with the employer before your start date, don't bet that the situation will improve after you start.

CHAPTER 10

Relational Interview Skills

Group Discussion and Personal Interview is an important process in selecting people for different positions in any organisation. In the present competitive environment, having domain knowledge in a particular subject is not enough, for getting a good job. Ability to effectively communicate, ideas, right body language, problem solving, analytical and relational (interpersonal) skills is essential and prerequisite to achieve the goal.

This book aims to equip all with various important skills as follows:

1. Influencing
2. Persuading
3. Delegating
4. Coaching
5. Praising
6. Presenting
7. Handling Conflict
8. Facilitating
9. Leading Team Meeting
10. Thinking Skills
11. Positive Thinking
12. Improve Your Memory
13. Blocks to Thinking
14. Logical Thinking
15. Creative Thinking
16. Brainstorming
17. Decision—Taking

There are eight to ten more skills but we will discuss here in short in the following manner: -

1. Influencing

What does "influencing" mean? An obvious place to start is with dictionary of functions. Influencing is defined by various dictionaries as:

- The ability to change someone's views, attitude or behaviours in a positive way.
- The power of a person to have an effect on someone else resulting from ability, wealth, position etc.

When considering what it means to influence, it is important to note that some definitions of leadership refer explicitly to influencing as an integral part of leadership. For example, in his text book on Management and Organizational behaviour, Laurie Millers discusses what leadership means:

"It is difficult to generalize about leadership, but essentially it is a relationship through which one person influence the behaviour or actions of other people. This means that the process of leadership cannot be separated from the activities of groups and with effective team building."

Even where definitions of leadership don't explicitly refer to influencing, you can often find an implicit reference. Such as in this definition of leadership from US academic Warren Bennis: "People who know what they want and why they want if, and have the skills to communicate that, to others in a way that gains support." So how do you communicate in a way that "gains support."

Power and Influence

There may be occasions where you have felt that you have been tricked into doing something, or perhaps correct. Neither method tends to leave a good impression of the person who has done the tricking or the coercion. It could be said that this person exerted influence but it is not likely to be the kind of influence, which is sustainable. People do not like being coerced or tricked. So how can we affect the behaviour of another person by influencing in a more positive manner? We will think of some specific skill areas later built first a word about sources of power. One definition of influence refers to the power someone has to affect another person's behaviour attitude. Power can be thought of in a number of ways, each relevant to the way leaders can influence others.

Three ways you can think of Power are:

1. Position Power: This is power that someone has because of their position in the organisation.
2. Expert Power: This is power based on someone is expertise their skills and knowledge.
3. Person Power: This is power that someone has because of how others think of them. If they are respected, valued and trusted then people are far more likely to listen and respond positively to them.

Think about your own situation and the possible power sources you have available. How can you build your own personal power based on these points?

Although a leader may well have a mix of each, the third power source is particularly interesting in the context of inter personal communication skills. A person can have power to influence other largely because they have developed trust and credibility with those they seek to influence.

Alongside these motions of power there are a number of skills that can develop to help you to influence more effectively.

Here we will consider:

- Active listening
- Being interested in others
- Aware of body language
- Assertiveness
- Building Rapport

Active listening and being interested in others

Active listening can be defined as:

"The act of alert international hearing, interpretation, and demonstration of an interest in what a person has to say through verbal signal, non-verbal gestures, and body language."

How does active listening relate to your ability influence? Because a key part of person power is being respected, valued and trusted, and to do this you need to be understood. And if you want to be better understood, first you need to understand others better. Take for instance this insight from the Danish philosopher and theologist Soren Kierkegaard:

"In order to help another effectively, I must understand what he understands. If I do not know that my greater understanding will be of no help to him instruction begins when you put yourself in his place so that you may understand what he understands and in the way he understands it."

Putting yourself in the shoes of others is a potent example of active listening, but it also suggests the second of the influencing skills, that of being interested in others, when others sense you are interested in them, and interested in their views, they are far more likely to respect and listen to yours. In many ways this is what US leadership Writer, Jay Conger expresses in his own, assessment of what makes an effective leader:

"The most effective leaders study the issues that matter to their colleagues in conversation they collect essential information.

They are good at listening. They test their ideas, with trusted confidents, and they ask questions of the people they will later be persuading. These explorations help them to think through the arguments, the evidence, and the prospective they will present."

Body language and being assertive

Being aware of your body language is another critical element of influencing your demeanour, movements and actions are all fundamentally important to influencing skills. Body language matters. Why? Because before you open your mouth to say anything your body has already spoken volumes. Various researchers suggest that upwards of 50% of our communication is by our body language. A dictionary definition for body language is:

- The conscious and unconscious movements and postures by which attitudes and feelings are communicated.

A key aspect of effective body language congruence

You are behaving in a congruent way when what you say mirrors your body language. We are all surprisingly good at noticing when someone is not being very convincing, usually when their body language does not backup their words. When it comes to what we believe, body language is far more convincing than the words people say.

This is particularly important for a leader attempting to convey confidence and assurance. Getting your body language right will encourage trust and help you influence and thus lead. All of these aspects of body language combined lead to positively and assertiveness, another key interpersonal skill.

Assertiveness in defined as:

- Communicating your views and feelings in a calm, direct and respectful way whilst respecting equally the views of others.

Building rapport

The mutual respect implicit in assertiveness helps to create trust and is an important aspect of building rapport. Building rapport is defined as:

- A sustained relationship of mutual understanding or trust and agreement between people.

Rapport exists when two people develop a mutual feeling of understanding, harmony, well-being and security. It is the result of an open and trusted relationship. Rapport is also about meeting people at their level, ensuring they are comfortable with you.

Both verbal and non-verbal body languages have a key role to play in this. An important aspect of rapport is empathizing with people's view points. When you have rapport with someone you feel of ease and condensations tend to flow. Influencing then becomes almost a natural consequence of having built a rapport with others. It is when influencing seems to be at its most natural that it is probably at its most effective.

Influencing skills summary

Influencing skills are a combination of various inter-personal skills. When brought together, these can help you to be effective in changing someone's views attitudes or behaviours, in a positive way. How effective are you at influencing other?

Sources of Power to influence:

- Which sources of power can you use to influence;
- Position Power;
- Export Power;
- Personal Power.

Active listening and being interested:

- Giving time to other to listen;
- Demonstrated you are interested. Body language and assertiveness:
- How does your body language demonstrate you are confident and assured;

- Putting your views forward confidently whilst valuing and recognizing other people's position and views.

Building Rapport:

- Mutual understanding and trust;
- Emphasizing with other people is view points.

2. Persuading

While the previous section focused an indirect ways to influence others, it is also important to develop your powers of Persuasion. Effective leadership often requires such direct methods to influence those we lead, Persuasion is defined as : the act or process of persuading someone to do or believe something. But how do you set about persuading someone? This is by no means a new question. Indeed, in some ways it is one that the ancient Greek philosopher Aristotle is said to have addressed.

Ethos logos and pathos

Here, Aristotle is said to have separated the means of persuading someone into three kinds of "appeals":

- An appeal to "Ethos"—the credibility of the person making the persuasive argument. How convinced are you by the person.
- An appeal to "Logos"—the use of logic to support a claim. Do the facts stack up?
- An appeal to "pathos"—the emotional or motivational appeal. Does the argument appeal to the emotions? Language choice can affect people's emotional response.

However, do not confuse open and honest persuasiveness with other, more negative ways to influence.

For example, contrast persuasion with two other ways to change a person's view:

- Propaganda, which tends to be ideologically driven and an ethically questionable approach to influencing.
- Manipulation, which suggests coercive attitudes of actions.

Persuasion should be seen as neutral, in the sense that it is not seeking to be ideologically driven or coercive.

Arguing if you are right, listening as if you are wrong

Stanford University Professor Bolesutton argues that leaders should adopt this approach to influencing:

Argue as if you are right; listen as if you are wrong

The two sides of this approach mirror the motion of advocacy and inquiry. Advocacy is making your thinking process visible.

"Here is my view and this how I arrived at the view."

In relation to developing your interpersonal skills, advocacy is about:

- Making your point taking a position in an attempt to influence others.
- Supporting your viewpoint with how you came to that view, whilst remaining open to alternative views.

On the other hand, inquiry means as king orders to make their thinking process visible.

"How does it sound to you? What makes sense to you and what does not?"

Inquiry is about:

- How questions are raised and answered.
- Allowing people to inquire into one another's reasoning and understand the conclusion they have reached.

Advocacy and inquiry are two sides of being persuasive. You make your best case for what you think is right, doing so as convincingly as possible. But you do this whilst listening very carefully to those around you, and being willing to change your view as a result.

Selling a Message

Being persuasive also means being able to sell a message. This is an important aspect of persuasiveness for a number of reasons. Selling a message can means:

- Convincing colleagues of a particular approach.
- Bringing employees on-board with your ideas.
- Persuading customers to buy your services or products.

Let us consider selling a message with respect to your customers. There is an old adage that people buy from people. So building your relationship and rapport with customers is a crucial skill. How do you do that? First try building your credibility by selling your own strengths. Such as:

- Your competence
- Your experience
- Your track record

Next you need to be clear about distinguishing between features and benefits. There is another sales adage: people buy benefits not features. So what are the differences?

- Features—describe a fact or characteristic of a service, what the service is:
- Benefits—are something customers have said they want what the service will do for them.

Often there is a tendency to talk "features" rather than finding out benefits from the client.

How do you know if you are talking about features rather than benefits? Here is one test:

- If you can come up with a sensible reply to "So what?" then you are probably talking features.
- If you can name the features then follow if with "so this means...," then you are talking benefits.

Being truly persuasive means focusing on benefits. So how do you avoid the "features trap"?

Here is a simple 3 step process:

1. Ask the client enough questions to discover what it is they need from you.
2. Link what the customer wants to the specific features of your offering which match those benefits.
3. Use the phrase "which means that" to convert features to benefits, whilst these points apply especially to customers they are equally valid-when cleaning with colleagues and employees. It is highly likely that they will be far more convinced by benefits than they will by features. And remember that whilst we most of us may claim to be logical, the real picture can be much less clear.

As Dale Carnegie once put it

"When dealing with people, remember you are not dealing with creatures of logic, but with creatures of emotion, creatures with prejudices and motivated by pride and vanity."

Persuasion Skills Summary

The following table provides a brief summary of the main points we have discussed about persuasion. Think about how you can become more persuasive in your inter-personal communication. Your appeal-ethos, logos and pathos

- Ethos—do you have credibility? How can you build your credibility?
- Logos—do the facts stack up? How can you build a convincing argument?
- Pathos—does your message appeal to the emotions? How can you discover what is important to people, things that matter to them?

Balancing advocacy and inquiry:

- Argue your view convincingly, as if you are right.
- Listen intensity to other views, as if you are wrong. Selling the message :
- Build your credibility, people buy from people.
- Focus on benefits rather than features.
- Ask, both clients and colleagues, sufficient questions—so that you know what they need.

How can you develop your powers of persuasion in the workplace?

Think about times when you have found other people to have been particularly persuasive. What persuaded you? How did they do it?

3. Delegating

At first thought it may seem strange to consider delegation as a communication skill for leaders. It is more usually understood as a management task. However, some of the critical steps in effective delegation are also crucial communication skills. When delegation goes wrong, it is often due to in effective or a complete breakdown in communication. Here we will consider the particular communications skills which are associated with delegation, including:

- Building trust.
- Communicating what is expected.
- Giving a clear brief.
- Encouraging questions.
- Providing support encouragement and giving feedback.

Perhaps the best way to consider communication skills in relation to delegation is to relate them to the steps and stages of delegation.

Delegation Defined

Firstly, what do we mean by delegation? Delegation is giving responsibility to someone to carry out tasks that you might normally do yourself. By delegating you give others the authority to do things, but you remain accountable for the outcome.

To understand delegation it is useful to answer some key questions:

- How do you give responsibility to someone else?
- How do you ensure they feel clear about what they are being asked to do?
- How do you support and encourage those to whom you have delegated responsibility?

Why Delegate

Before considering the "how" questions above, perhaps we need to answer an even more pressing question. Why delegate in the first place? There is a common tendency for leaders to try and keep hold of tasks, activities and processes. What is wrong with this? Well, the famous industrialist Andrew Carriage provided a powerful answer to these questions:

"No person will make a great business who wants to do it all himself or get all the credit." This quote from Carnegie makes two good points. Firstly, to grow you need to trust other people to get important things done. Secondly, when you do delegate and someone is doing the tasks really well, give them the credit for what they are doing.

Delegation also matters at a practical level. If:

- Releases your time to concentrate on other key tasks.
- Develops the capability of others in your team.

Leader delegate both to give themselves more time to load, and crucially to help other to develop and grow in their abilities and responsibilities.

How do you delegate?

Done well, delegation is an invaluable tool for leaders. However, to do it well we must think of it as a process. This includes several stages and proper use of a set of communication skills.

Combining these will help ensure that delegation is effective.

The 5 stages of effective delegation are:

1. Identify the person:
   - Trust the other person and builds trust
   - Apply the willing and able test do they want to do the task and have they the capability to do it?
2. Select the Task:
   - Match the right person to the task, and their development needs.
   - Do not delegate just the mundane. Delegate activities are worthwhile and valuable.
   - But do delegate less important tasks allowing you more time to focus on the important.
   - Think about delegating tasks to others in your team who have strengths in areas that you might not possess, others may have strengths where you have weaknesses.
3. Clarify Expectations:
   - Outline what is expected and what needs to be achieved. Make sure you clarify how this task fits with other things that are being done and why it matters.
   - Specify the outcome and key things that need to be achieved. Let the individual work out how they will achieve this.
   - Give a clear briefing.
4. Provide Support, Encouragement and Feedback:
   - Encourage questions, continue to be available and plan to monitor and review progress.
   - Review initially in a supportive manner, then less frequently over time as the individual's expertise increases. Do not be "Looking over someone's shoulder" all the time.
   - Provide support appropriate to your colleague is need. Avoid the two extremes sometimes associated with poor delegation.
   - Either of abdicating your own responsibility to support, or of being over-bearing, retaining to much control.

5. Review:
   - Did the delegation activity result in you being free to focus on other important leadership tasks?
   - How did the person to whom you delegated develop? Have they increased their own capability and expertise?
   - What lessons have you learned from delegating?

Here is why it is best to leave others to work out how to do something:

"Never tell people how to do things. Tell them what to do and they will surprise you with their ingenuity. General George Smith Patton, Jor. The 5 stages for delegation provide a structured set of steps to follow. They identify what is needed to be done. However, understanding how to delegate means focusing on the communication skills needed.

Communication skill for delegation

In the following table the range of communication skills needed for delegation are highlighted on the left hand side.

Identify the person:

- Building trust and understanding;
- Listening and questioning to individual an individual's strengths

Select the task:

- Discussion of Development needs to identify opportunities.
- Self-reflection to recognize what best to delegate.
- Conversations about what tasks to delegate.

Clarify expectations:

- Clarify what is required and expected.
- Specify the outcome and key things, which need to be achieved. But does not detail how it should be done where appropriate; allow freedom for the individual to work out how they might achieve the outcome.

Provide support and encouragement:

- Encourage questions to ensure undertaking.
- Balance support with allowing the individual to get on with their tasks;

- Be available and listen;
- Provide feedback and encouragement

Review:

- Discuss with the individual how they feel they have developed;
- Ask for feedback on your own role and performance. In what ways did you help?

Delegation quick checklist

Finally here is a quick checklist to help you manage the communication of delegation. You can also use this checklist as a way to review how you have delegated by adding comments to the stages.

Who—identify the person and match the person to the task, their capability and development needs.

What—Select the task, or project.

Who—Brief clearly, and agree SMART objectives. Next—Provide support as appropriate and be available.

P/P—set up mini-reviews to discuss progress, issues and plans (PIP)

As a final thought on delegation consider the words of Theodore Roosevelt:

"The best executive is the one who has sense enough to pick good men to do what he wants done, and self-restraint enough to keep from meddling with them while they do it."

4. Coaching

There will be many occasions where a colleague does not feel they are capable of having a particular task delegated to them, or it may be the first time they have experienced the delegation process. In both of these situations what might be needed is coaching support. In the first scenario, your colleague may need coaching to develop their ability to handle the task. In the second, they may need coaching to help them understand how delegation works.

There may be several other reasons, why someone needs coaching. Perhaps to help with:

- New skill development.
- Confidence building.

- Understanding a process
- A way of reflecting on and improving their practice.
- Support during the management of a change programme in the organization.
- To develop as a leader.
- Career development.

A coaching need is a development need. Such needs tend to be fairly specific and are lest addressed with clear goals or focus.

What is coaching?

Coaching is a process which supports people in developing their skills and achieving their goals;

This is done by helping people:

- Set mutually agreed goals.
- Identify activities and ways to develop their skills abilities and experience.
- Plan and then review what they have done, by using questions and providing feedback.

There are several approaches to coaching though there tends to be broad agreement that all involve:

- Activities to develop someone's skills and abilities.
- Adopting non-directive approaches to development, through there are differing views about the extent to which coaching may be directive.
- Focusing on improving performance.
- Developing goals that are both organizational and individual.
- Providing feedback on both strengths and weaknesses.

It is suggested that the roots of the term coaching date back to around 1830, in one of the most famous universities in the world, Oxford University. The word, coach was used as slag for a tutor who "carries" a student through an exam. It now means something different, conveying more the sense of supporting people to get from where they are to where they want to be. This motion still expresses much that is central to coaching.

More recently coaching has been defined as:

- Guiding people toward letter performance.
- The process of guiding the larger through an experience, as opposed to directing the learner through the experience.

- A coach "sets mutually agreed targets with individuals and teams, plans how to achieve them, then delegates the authority to get on with it and monitors but does not intervene in reality—the "eyes on the hands off approach" (Bole Garratt).
- Coaching is about performing at your best through the individual and private assistance of someone who will challenge, stimulate and guide you to keep growing.

It is also possible and useful to contrast coaching with training and mentoring. These activities may be related and can overlap, but it is also easy to confuse them. Here are some key differences between training, mentoring and coaching:

- **Training**—is a more explicit definition of knowledge and skills usually led by the trainer. It involves instructional techniques used to aid learning.
- **Mentoring**—is a more open two way exchange, with less specific goals, usually promoted by the mentor. It involves broad discussion, with the mentor acting as a guide. Mentors often act as signposts, suggesting areas to address making introductions ferments to discuss points with others.

The 5 P's of Coaching

One useful way to think about coaching into use the 5 P's approach The 5 P's of coaching include:

- **Preparation**—deciding together on what should be discussed at the coaching session. Gathering information and where possible objective evidence of progress to date. Reviewing the previous discussion plans.
- **Presence**—making sure as a coach that you give undivided attention, conveying that the coaching session is important, and listening attentively.
- **Practice**—planning how new skills, knowledge and behaviours can be practiced to develop competence and confidence.
- **Play-back**—provide feedback on how someone is progressive and developing.
- **Perform**—the aim of coaching is to see someone apply their skills in activities that make a contribution to the performance of the team and the organization.

How do they have an impact on performance? Done properly, coaching is a very effective way to help people develop. Coaching requires leaders to provide people with regular contact, explore their progress and help them to decide how to develop further.

Communication skills for coaching

Coaching is an involved and-skilful process. It assumes the coach has some practical experience and appreciation of how to learn and develop performance. That is not to say that the coach needs to be an expert in the actual tasks but rather being skilled in how learning is transferred into practice. There is a wide range of communication skills that are important to effective coaching. To coach effectively leaders need to develop their own skills in several areas. These include:

- **Questing**: Coaches raise questions at a number of levels and for a variety of purposes.
- **Preliminary:** Seeking initial information and clarification of facts and feeling. This is mainly descriptive.
- **Probing:** Progressing to probing analytical questions. Asking questions might challenge performance.
- **Possibilities:** Asking "future" and "possibility" questions. Questions that identify what next or how good performance can be built on. These questions can also explore where more development is needed and how these and subsequent improvement might be achieved.
- **Active listening:** Applying active listening skills to demonstrate that the coach is really "there" for the person being coached. Confirming they are listening, paying attentions to what is said and to body language being used?
- **Summarising:** A powerful technique that does more than just check understanding. Check your understanding of what the person, you are coaching, has said. Summarising allows the other person to hear what you think they have said. They can then more clearly reflect on what they mean, and what has been understood. This often results in fresh insight or prompts more in depth discussion.
- **Setting Goals:** Coaching conversations should be based on mutually agreed goals. These are bash led by the person being coached, so that they "own" the goals. The coach needs to help the person they are coaching to identify goals that they find challenging and stimulating. Then ensure that they are specific, so that it is clear what success means and of when it will be achieved.

- **Discussion:** Two-way conversation to explore issues, possibilities and approaches to developing skills. Looking for opportunities to develop skills and reflecting on experiences.
- **Giving Feedback:** Providing your view on how someone is progressing. As for as possible, feedback should be based on objective evidence. There is a more defined discussion of this topic in a later section.

A Coaching Process

There is a variety of coaching processes which can be used to help structure a coaching assignment.

Most of them end to follow a common management process:

- Reviewing what has been done.
- Planning what needs to be done.
- Doing, Putting those plans into action, coaching is often about achieving a balance between challenge and support.

The coaching skill is often about recognizing when to challenge or stretch the person you are coaching, and when to provide support and encouragement perhaps when they are struggling or finding things difficult of course, it is easier to accept challenges and be willing to stretch your abilities when you feel supported, so the two approaches actually go hand-in- hand. This approach to coaching is sometimes referred to as being a "critical friend." Keep holding the tension between a trusted friend and someone who is willing to provide an honest critique.

Of course, effective coaching is about being flexible and labouring your approach to soil the particular person being coached and the particular circumstances being addressed. For example, sometimes you may need to spur someone on to stretch them, and to challenge them to try something new, or to improve further. Alternatively someone you are coaching may need support or help when they are struggling with a particular issue. Or encouragement to step back and take a wider perspective about a particular issue that has logged them down. A process to give structure to coaching helps a coach to apply the communications skills discussed in the previous section, whilst continually balancing challenge and support. However, another important practice in coaching is the adoption of different coaching styles.

Coaching styles

The style of coaching support given or needed often varies, dependent in a few common factors:

- The capability of the person being coached.
- The preferences of the coach.
- The nature of the skills being coached.

There is a spectrum of styles used by coaches, typically based on the four summarized below.

At one end of the spectrum there is a relatively structured approach, which is led by the coach.

At the other end the person being coached has much more freedom to decide what to do. The four coaching styles are:

Instructional Coach:

- More structured coaching with a directive approach, where the coach leads and sets the agenda;
- Often used when new skills are being introduced and the person being coached is relatively in-experienced;
- Also used where the task/activities are more prescriptive in nature.

Trainer Coach:

- Showing by example;
- This is a less-directive approach, but still quite hands on;
- Requires the coach to be proficient in the activities;
- Coach is recognized as a role model.

Stimulator Coach:

- Balancing support and challenge;
- Mutual responsibility for goal seething;
- Coach encourage, stimulates development;
- Prompts the person being coached to propose options.

Synergistic Coach:

- The person being coached is often capable and takes the load;
- Coach looks for synergies, how the person being coached can be helped by networks, and access to wider resources;
- "Sounding board" and "critical friend" tend to be important roles for the coach in this style;
- This style has overlaps with mentoring.

5. Praising

In the previous section we discussed one important skill for effective coaching providing feedback. Feedback can be used to give information or praise, but it is also extremely useful as a tool to help people to improve. Typically, it has two main purposes:

1. **To Motivate:** When team members are performing well, feedback can increase confidence and encourage them to continue at level of performance.
2. **To Correct:** When team members are not performing as well as you would like, feedback can help determine how to change and improve their performance. Good quality feedback can achieve a number of things. For example, if:
    - Improves performance
    - Helps motivation
    - Boosts confidence
    - Develops skills and understanding
    - Shows people you value them

Feedback is used is a wide range of leadership and management activities.

It is critical when:

- Providing coaching support.
- Conducting performance management reviews and appraisals.
- Engage in more general, one to one discussions
- Reviewing how well a delegated activity is progressing
- Handling conflict
- Facilitating

Praising is amazing the power of feedback as a motivational tool Feedback is very much a part of organizational life, yet one aspect of giving feedback is often under used and undervalued. It is also an aspect of feedback that has considerable potential. Feedback can be a simple yet powerful motivational tool. Just by praising people for what they have done leaders can have a galvanizing effect. It is strange that something so effective yet simple is so rarely or poorly done. Giving praise is a simple, two-step process:

1. Look out for the behaviours and practice you want to see.
2. As soon as you see what you want to encourage, make sure you praise the person.

Essentially, apprising is giving people positive feedback, reinforcing and supporting good performance.

Too often we are quick to point out weakness or where things are going wrong, and slow to praise what is done well.

Tips for giving positive feedback

Thinks about the value of giving positive feedback with these tips:

Praise:

Praising people for what is done well, is for more powerful then criticizing for what was not done well.

Catch-people:

- "Catch people" doing what you want to see? Make if public:
- Give positive feedback openly and publicly.

A simple practice:

- Make this simple act of praising a routine part of your practice. Important Performance:
- If you want to see performance levels increase, this is one of the simplest and most powerful things you can do.

Quick and Slow:

- Be quick to praise, slow to blame, of course, it is important to ensure your praise is appropriate and in proportion to what has been achieved. This means what you say will be credible, valid and worthwhile. The ideal of positive feedback is captured well by Blaise Pascal when he said:

"Kind words do not cost much. They never blister the tongue or lips. They make other people good natured.

They also produce their own image on men's souls and a beautiful image it is."

Effective feedback

So, by far the most important kind of feedback to give someone is positive feedback. Of course you will also need to give feedback where you want people to correct or improve their performance.

There are some good general tips for ensuring that feedback achieves this purpose. To be effective, all feedback should be :

- Specific
- Descriptive and focused on actions not the person
- Honest and sincere
- Fair and accurate
- Future Oriented: This is particularly important for corrective feedback of course, not all feedback is necessarily positive.

There are always accessions when more difficult feedback needs to be provided. Here are some tips to bear in mind when providing corrective feedback

1. Outline the performance area that needs attention and explain why the existing performance is causing concern.
2. Discuss and explore the reasons for the person's current performance and show that you clearly understand the situation.
3. Ask if they have any suggestions on how to overcome any issues, and on ways to improve performance.
4. Ask what you can do to help.
5. Agree a mutual action plan for you both to take forward, and set a definite follow-up date.

Feedback is a vital skill for leaders and managers. Don't forget that:

- People tend to want to know how well they are doing.
- The purpose of providing feedback is to improve performance.
- It's always best to keep the two kinds of feedback separate. If you are going to praise someone them do so, but not at the same time as providing corrective feedback. People will tend to only remember what they perceive as negative.
- You should try to ensure that you praise more than you correct. Tim Walter Stone, the founder of UK based book retailer Water stone's Captures what he considers to be the link between positive feedback and leadership:

"I believe that the mindset that allows you to spend your working life thanking and congratulating people rather than being unpleasant to them is the mainstay of good leadership."

6. Presenting

One area that can be a challenge for many people is delivering a presentation. For some, this can be especially problematic when the situation really matters. Think about pressure situations where you might be required to present. For example, presenting to:

- The Chief Executive or senior management team in your organization.
- A critical client meeting, presenting to win an important contract.
- To a hostile and anxious group of employees, perhaps worried about their jobs.
- At an interview for a job you really want whatever the context the purpose of presentations is to send and receive information, but to do it in a way that makes people want to hear what you say.

Getting your Message Across

Getting your message across is more than just saying the right things, though that would be a useful start. Think about the last time you delivered a presentation. Reflect on what went well, and what did not go so well.

The start-point for getting your message across is to consider these critical questions:

Firstly, what is the purpose of your presentation?

When you have answered that, try being more specific by asking:

- Are you trying to influence?
- Are you delivering a starting?
- Are you trying to sell an idea?
- Are you trying to sell yourself? (At a job interview for example)
- Are you proposing a plan?
- Are you reporting on a project?
- Are you facilitating a group?
- Are you running a training session?

Presentations can be used for a wide variety of purposes. Knowing why you are presenting gives you clarify on what you need to say and how you might say it.

To get your message across effectively, it's useful to consider these two perspectives:

- Firstly, what do you want to say?
- Secondly, what do you think those present have come to hear?

Dale Carnegie, the famous US writer on public speaking once said:

"There are always three speeches for everyone who actually gave. The one you practiced the one you gave, and the one you wished you gave."

There is a fourth that could be added to Carnegie's list:

- The one the audience received.

It is worth remembering that different parts of your presentation will appeal to different groups of your audience.

Beginning and Ending

When we are asked about our experience of a service it is interesting to note how we respond. Research from the behavioural sciences suggests that some things matter more than others. For example, how do customers experience the passage of time and interpret events after they are over?

- People remember beginnings well.
- Ending is remembered better than beginnings and have a bigger impact on customers.
- Positive peaks within the service contribute to customer satisfaction.

Clearly, beginnings matter. So in preparing your presentation, spend plenty of time making sure that you start well. A good beginning will both give you confidence for the rest of the presentation, and engage the audience.

It seems that endings matter even more than beginnings. Many presenters will finish with a summary or re-cap but try to go beyond that. Plan to end on a high, sending you audience away both well-informed and motivated.

The 60 second test

One way to start outlining your presentation is to ask yourself some initial questions. Starting with 60 seconds test:

- If you only had 60 seconds to get your messages across, what would the headlines be?
- What is the title of the presentation?—The title may give you a steer or a theme.
- What do you want people to be able to do at the end of the presentation? What result do you want to achieve.

- What is the purpose of the presentation—to sell, to influence, to persuade, to report back?
- What information could you provide in another way? Curiosity-raising questions, handling out information in a fact sheet at the end.
- Who do you need to communicate with?

Presentation checklist

The 60 seconds test will give you some initial thoughts for your presentation but for really effective presentations you need a process. Use this four-stage check list to help you develop and deliver an effective presentation.

Plan:

- Describe the audience.
- Define the purpose of the presentation

Try the 60 second test Prepare:

- Establish a positive mind set;
- Opening-grade attention;
- Illustrate key points and use visuals;

Prepare a memorable close. Practice:

- Become comfortable with your message and your incidence engagement and approach;
- Pay special attention to practicing your beginning and end. First and last impressions count.

Present:

- "Own" the subject;
- Make a positive first impression;
- Build Rapport;
- Hold attention
- Thrive to continuously improve.

"An effective speaker knows that the success or failure of his talk is not for him to decide—it will be decided in the minds and hearts of his hearers." Dale Carnegie.

7. Handling Conflict

Handling conflict at work is a never carry. It is something few people like to deal with, yet it is a vital aspect of the manager's role.

Leaving conflicts unsolved can affect morale and destabilize the working environment. Not just for those at the centre of the conflict but often for the team around them.

What is the Problem?

The first step in handling conflict is to be aware of the possible reason behind the conflict.

There a numerous reasons why conflicts emerge, including:

- Personal clashes
- Misunderstandings
- Differences in values
- Poor communication
- Misuse of power
- Bullying Behaviour
- Feelings of injustice over real or perceived unfair treatment.

By definition some conflicts are easier to handle than others. Some can be resolved with straight forward intervention. In other cases you may need the support of your line managers of HR team. To help you decide which route to conflict resolution is best it is important to consider the different types of response.

Typical responses to conflict

Firstly, conflict is not necessarily a bad thing.

There are bound to be disagreements between people at work and, if dealt with constructively, the outcomes can be very positive, Dealing with conflict can clear the air, and it can also help surface differences which may make everyone think differently. It can also contribute to better understanding of each other.

Whilst conflict can lead to positive outcomes, typically we are not very good at handling it. This might especially be the case where we are unused to dealing with conflict, or are fearful of its consequences.

For this reason, most people will have a preferred way of dealing with difficult situations. A good place to start thinking about communication skills in handling conflict is recognizing that there are different ways that people behave. There are a number of ways in which people instinctively deal with conflict at work. *For example:*

Avoiding:

- But you will have to live with the conferences; Giving in;
- May resolve the conflict but for how long, and what cost? Something over;
- A compromise which might leave neither side happy; Arguing :
- Responding argumentatively takes energy and is likely to be confrontational;

Solving together:

- Working together to solve the conflict is a constrictive, mutual way forward. You could argue that all five responses can have their place.
- Avoiding conflict might be all that you can cope with at the moment. Perhaps there is too much else on at the time, so this approach allows you to cope, albeit temporarily.
- Giving in might be workable because you just want the situation resolved and need to move on.
- Something it over could be an accommodation that you decide is good enough.
- Arguing could work in that it allows you to say exactly what you do think about the situation and gets if "off your chest."
- Solving together, not surprisingly, is the approach advocated.

However, whilst some responses may enable you to cope with a given circumstance, using the first four approaches will depend on the exact nature of the conflict. Repeated use of these responses could be detrimental. By far the best approach is to cultivate behaviours which enable you to adopt the fifth approach: working together to solve the conflict. Here is why

Solving conflict together

The first two approaches suggest a passive response to conflict.

- **Avoiding Conflict:** Whilst avoiding conflict may at first seem the least damaging way forward, it can often lead to feelings of frustrating and anger.
- **Giving in:** To give in suggests that you do not or cannot face the challenge of resolving the conflict. More often than not, giving in can result in feelings of resentment and frustration.

The second two approaches require more engagement with the conflict.

- **Smoothing Over:** To smooth over a conflict means that you have at least recognized that there is a conflict. The act of smoothing over means there is at least some engagement with conflicting parties, and that you have decided to address it by compromise.
- **Responding argumentatively**—In contrast to smoothing things over, responding argumentatively typically assumes the position of being right in the conflict whilst this can reveal insights into the conflict itself, and those in conflict, unchecked or uncontrolled arguing can prolong, escalate or worsen the situation.

The final approach is built upon mutual engagement.

Work together to solve the conflict this approach predominantly means adopting a problem solving mind set. This seeks understanding options and resolution by engaging all parties. Typically working together to solve the conflict involves a five stage process:

Gaining Clarity:

- About what the conflict is actually about; Other People' Shoes:
- Seeing things from the other person perspective; Your View:
- Putting your perspective forward; Possible resolutions:
- Identifying possible resolutions to the conflict that both parties can accept;

Agree progress:

Agreeing a way forward together

Successfully handling a conflict means applying typical management skills, such as problem solving earlier in this book. Active listening body language, building support and influencing must all be employed.

Important as your general management skills may be, the way you communicate can also significantly affect the outcome of a conflict.

Remember That:

"Whenever you are in conflict with someone, there is one factor that can make the difference between damaging your relationship and deepening it. That factor is attitude." (William James US Philosopher)

8. Facilitation

How often do you come away from meetings or away—days/ off-sites with the feeling that things just got harder and instead of progress you come away feeling you have taken several steps back. What in the answer?

Effective facilitation

What is facilitation?

Facilitation is often seen as a neutral role, using guidance and encouragement takes to help team members to achieve the objectives of the meeting. However, properly used, there is nothing neutral about, the potential power of effective facilitation. It can do more than help the team to meet objectives.

Using a structured facilitation approach can help bring out the best in any team:

Facilitation skills are at a premium. Whether it is a team meeting, an away day offsite, or a conference, the effectiveness of such events is often determined by how well they are facilitated. That difference can make all the differences. For example, think about the value gained when:

- Everyone feels involved and engaged in a meeting on how to take thing forward.
- Ideas are allowed or encouraged to flow at a meeting.
- You leave a meeting feeling it had purpose and direction, and it achieved something.
- A clear set of actions are agreed and everyone feels motivated to make them happen.

Facilitation helps to get the best from any meeting. It can help prevent:

- Meetings that feel like you do nothing but go round in cycles.
- A hi-jack situation, where the loud little dominates or disrupts.

- An important problem never really getting resolved because nobody has conducted a structured analysis of the problem.

You can also think of facilitation as the art and science of helping groups in their thinking, planning and decision-making. Too often we do not realise the knowledge and potential that we have within the team or group of people that we have brought together in many cases, the insights and knowledge needed to solve problems or identify innovative ways forward are already there in the organization. The skill to unlock that knowledge and expertise is often found in the form of facilitation.

Facilitation: Focus on progress

How can facilitation make so much of a difference? To answer that, the definition of the word is instructive in itself.

Facilitation is:

- To make action and processes easier
- To help forward or to help progress Good facilitation makes things easier, and helps to make progress.

There are three main elements to effective facilitation:

- Interpersonal skills
- Focus on progress;
- Personal characteristics.

If you can combine these effectively, then you will be in a position to reap the benefits of resourceful people gathered together is a team setting. Next we will conserve each of these in turn.

Facilitation—Making Progress

The key challenge of facilitation is to ensure progress is achieved. To do this you need to focus on the event you are facilitating. Well is not easy. The first and foremost task when facilitating is to progress towards the aim and goal of the meeting or event. To do this you need to:

- Ensure enthusiasm and meaningful intent is clearly conveyed, setting the meeting tone right from the start, and motivating those present.
- Manage the level of activity and engagement.
- Observe the energy levels at stages of the event and adjust the face accordingly provide a short break, or change of activity when energy levels are low.

- Help the group identity connections.
- Make sure feedback from group discussion is short and focused, avoid "death by feedback".

For example, ask sub groups to feedback three things they have discussed, or what they fell was most important.

- Acknowledge ideas and contribution, build a consensus.
- Build a balance between:
  - Initiating
  - Posing questions
  - Summarising;
  - Moving things on;
  - Keeping to time;
  - Concluding;
  - Managing people, contributions and involvement.

Interpersonal skills for facilitation

To manage progress you not only need to keep things on track, but just as importantly you need to use good interpersonal skills.

These include:

Building Rapport: We discussed rapport earlier in this book. In this context rapport is about meeting people of their level, ensuring they are comfortable with you. An important aspect of rapport is empathizing with people's view points and establishing credibility to enable people to contribute with ease.

Communicating effectively—both verbally and non-verbally Being supportive and using language that is familiar to the group so that you do not set yourself apart from the language you use. Body language will also indicate that you are attentive, positive, supportive, and engaged with their discussions.

Active listening–demonstrating your interest by confirmatory comments ("Yes I see," "go on" etc.)

And use body language which is open and demonstrates your interest. Each really matter, helping to set the tone and climate of the meeting or event.

Questioning Techniques—You can use questions as a very powerful facilitation skill. Use these to check understanding; ask for clarification, as for a view to be expanded. You can also ask questions to get people thinking differently.

Personal Characteristics

The third skill set for effective facilitation relates to personal characteristics. The first point fo make is perhaps an obvious one, but an important one nonetheless everyone is different.

Therefore everyone should play to their strengths and use their own personal characteristics to ensure they are effective.

So think about what you personally bring to the facilitating of a session. What individual strengths do you have that can help facilitate progress and make things easier? *For example,* think about your own:

- Ability for learning (before, during and after the meeting).
- Friendliness (but do not befalls or act unnaturally).
- Sensitivity
- Integrity
- Sense of humour
- Openness to change
- Self-awareness

Of course, whilst it is important to be self aware, do not forget to think about how others may perceive your personal characteristics an relation to each of these areas. To what extent does this affect your ability to facilitate or manage?

9. Leading Team Meeting

Team meetings—It has been said that there are only two kinds of activities in an organisation:

1. Attending meetings,
2. Answering the phone for others who are away attending meetings.

How often do we hear complaints that there are too many meetings, which are too long, and which are too badly run. Let meetings are crucial to the functioning of any team—as long as they are properly conducted. Being able to schedule and run a meeting is a crucial skill for any team leader. Why? Because:

A meeting in time saves nine.

Effective team meetings—why meet?

The starting point for leading effective team meetings is to understand them. This starts with this fundamental question.

Why meet? There are many valuable and valid reasons for scheduling a team meeting. They can be used to:

- consult by giving, or receiving advice;
- make decisions;
- share information;
- solve problems;
- generate creative ideas;
- enable face to face conflict;
- negotiate or influence;
- benefit from several minds, all focused on one problem;
- brief—for example, give information to the team;
- review—give a progress report;
- develop the team;
- Ensure the same message is given to all;
- Make effective use of time—but only if the meeting is led effectively.

So before calling a meeting, make sure you are clear in your own mind why you are calling it.

Ensure your meeting addresses some of the above reasons is a good place to start.

Types of meeting

Meetings may be formal or informal, formal meetings tend to be a part of the fabric of some organisations.

These may have written remits and be a part of a hierarchy of meetings where reports are tabled. Formal meetings will often consist of such things as:

- A pre-arranged meeting time or schedule.
- An agenda—a description of items to be discussed.
- A set of minutes—a written record of the issues discussed at the meeting.
- A chair person to lead, co-ordinate or control.
- An administrator or secretary—to keep a record of the meeting.
- An agreed process and procedure.

Alternatively, informal meetings typically do not require the same structure a processes. For example, informal meetings may involve:

- Being arranged randomly or at short notice.
- Unstructured discussion.
- No procedures or process,

- Any taking the lead.
- The noting of action points—things individuals agreed to do.

Effective team meetings; the basics rule number one only hold a meeting if it is absolutely necessary. If you are calling the meeting make sure it is really necessary. Could you achieve its objectives in any other way? Think about the cost in time, money and resource use. Do not manage your business with busyness!

If you are being called to a meeting, ask yourself: do you really need to attend? For many people, the number of meetings they are asked to attend can have a significant effect on the time they actually have to get things done. Even if it is your boss who has called the meeting, try to be objective? One of the most important elements of effective meetings is to ensure the right people are present. It might be useful to think of when we are inviting people to meetings:

- Who knows?
- We can?
- Who cares?

Only invite people who need to be present or who can make a worthwhile contribution.

Another key to effective team meetings is your reputation. Try to build a reputation for running meetings well. Think about the advice above. Involve and engage other, and try to use the meeting to make decisions that promote action.

One major concern with meetings is that they replace real work, and become talking shops with no action. Develop your meeting skills so that real work is achieved and facilitated, by running effective meetings. How do you do this?

Meetings tips-before, during and after

Meetings—the practical attentive to work: Before the meetings:

- Ensure you really need to meeting.
- Set specific, realistic achievable goals.
- Prepare and distribute an agenda and any (necessary) supporting documentation.
- Issue a start and finish time for the meeting;
- Estimate time for agenda items in advance.
- Invite only key people or team members, not everybody you can think of.

Be prepared. During:

- Start on time.
- Keep the team on track.
- Make decisions, do not just air views.
- Summarise and record decisions.
- Keep the team involved—remember they are there for a reason.
- Control dominating characters.

End on time. After:

- Send minutes to participate.
- Follow up agreed actions.
- Debrief with key figures.
- Assess the content of the meeting—what came out of it.
- Assess the process of the meeting—what needs to change from it.

Managing content and process

A useful way to think about a meeting is to distinguish between content and process. The content of the meeting refers to:

- Why has the meeting bean called?
- What needs to be done?
- Who should do it?
- When should be done?
- What information is needed?

The process of the meeting is about ensuring that:

- People's interactions are managed.
- Contributions are shared around the group.
- Agreement is active not passive.
- Digressions are managed.
- Decisions are made using fair decision making processes.

Facilitating team meetings

This is also a helpful way to think about facilitation skills. Effectively combining meeting content with essential process steps will help your teams gain the most from knowledge and skills, and to achieve agreed outcomes.

Leading team meetings effectively require a wide range of skills. These include the ability to focus on how meetings/workshops are progressing, blended with your own inter-personal skills, and your personal characteristics. Developing facilitation skills and combining these with team leadership is not easy. To become really good at both of these you need to :

— Build your knowledge base
— Think about what you are doing
— Then get plenty of practice

"Tell me and I will forget; show me and I may remember; involve me and I will understand." (Chinese proverb)

10. Thinking Skills

Using your Brain in the information Age

The potential of the brain

The facts about the brain are truly stupendous. For example, do you know that the human brain takes up a fifth of all the energy generated by your body in its resting state? It is similar to a 20- watt light bulb continuously glowing. How big do you think the brain is? Well, if you can imagine it, your brain consists of 100billion cells, each one of which connects to 1000 other brain cells making a total of 100,000 billion connections. There are more cell connection points in the human brain then there are stars in our galaxy. Norman Cousins had put it "Not even the universe with all its countless billions of galaxies represents greater wonder or complexity then the human brain."

Brain power

Here are some more astonishing facts about your brain. Although the brain weighs just 3 lb, it contains 12 trillion nerve cells more than two and a half times the people on this planet. It contains 1000 trillion trillion molecules (way beyond our ability to compute), and can process 30 billion bits of information a second. Your brain has 10 billion neurons and the range of connections all the neurons in the brain could make would amount to one with 28 noughts after it. Just stop and just stop and write that down to get a feel for what that is. Your brain has enough atomic energy to build any of the world's major cities many times over. Unsurprising no human being has yet existed who has been to use all the potential of the brain. How about you?

Exploding the Myths

One of the reasons we fail to make the most of our brain and, therefore, our thinking skills is that we hang on to a range of inherited assumptions about our brain and our capacity to think. Many of us believe that, contrary to the facts, we are either born bright or stupid. We think that we are only as intelligent as our measured Intelligence Quotient (IQ) and that this is fixed throughout our lives, we think that, when we run up against big problems, they just cannot be solved. We fret over taking decisions and bemoan our ability to choose wisely. We think that we are stuck with the way. We think and that we cannot change it. And top things off, we think that, as we age our brain declines and with it, out abilities to remember things. They only one of these assumptions that is true is that it is only our thinking that limits the power of our brains.

Brain works

A simple look at what we ask of our brains is enough to show as what a wonderful organ this is. First, unlike other species, we are the only species that can think in the 3 dimensions of past, present and future. We can use our brains to interpret our world in any way we chose, at one extreme, positively and, at the other, negatively. We can use our brains for working out answer to logical problems as well as using it imaginatively to work out answers to illogical problems. We can imagine without brains, invent and innovate. We can learn, change and develop. We can use our brains to interpret, understand, and become wise. We can use our brains to analyse things and to synthesise things. And, again, uniquely for species and this planet, we can use our brains to think about our thinking. The brain is truly the most complex and versatile tool we have in our bodies.

Brain not brawn

The wonderful instrument that our brains are, it astonishes that, until very, recently, thinking was regarded in industrialized countries as a second-class skill. For several centuries, people were employed first for their manual labour, secondly, for their machine-operating skill and lastly, and only it called upon, for their thinking ability. Today, all that has changed. We no longer live in an industrialized age but an information age. Instead of brawn, the successful companies and economies of today and the future need brains. They are the ones that will harness, use and reward the combined thinking abilities of everyone in them.

Management Thinking

So what kind of thinking skills do we need in the information Age? Mike Paddler and Tom Boydell are researches who have studied the qualities needed by successful workers. They found that at least half of the key skills are those that relate to how we use our brains.

Their list reads:

1. Command on basic facts.
2. Relevant professional understanding.
3. Continuing sensitivity to events.
4. Analytical, problem-solving, decision-talking and judgement making skills.
5. Social skills and abilities.
6. Emotional resilience.
7. Reactivity: an ability to respond purposefully to events.
8. Creativity.
9. Mental agility.
10. Balanced learning habits.
11. Self-knowledge.

Thinking matters

All of us are capable of developing our thinking in all those different skills. But we are slow to change. Percy Barnevik former chairman of ABB says, "Organisations ensure people only use 5 to 10% of their abilities at work. Outside of work, the same people engage the other 90 to 95%."

By contrast Jack Watch former CEO of General Electric says that encouraging ideas was one of his top three tasks. One of Welch's typical approaches was to ask his managers not only what their ideas were, but who they shared them with and who adopted them. When the factory of American entrepreneur and founder of IBM, Thomas Watson burnt down, Watson was surprisingly unified. When asked why, he said that the wealth of his business was not based in his offices assembly lines and buildings but in the intellectual capital of his employees. He said, "I can re-build the offices and buildings. But I could never replace the combined knowledge, abilities and thinking skills of my people."

Key points

1. The human brain is so powerful that few of us come anywhere near to using if as well as we could.
2. Every person has the ability to think intelligently and creatively.
3. The brain is the source of key mental facilities such as memory, imagination, creativity and innovation.
4. The brain is the key tool for mastering the modern information age.
5. Everyone is a modern organization is a knowledge worker to some extent.
6. According to research, half the skills needed by successful workers involve the use of thinking skills.

11. Positive Thinking

For much of the time our thoughts let us down. They are confused, disjointed and reactive. They do not have to be. Through training our thoughts to be positive, focused and assertive, we can at a stroke improve the quality of our thinking.

Untrained thinking

When we treat the brain as an unknown quantity that we cannot manage, then our untrained thinking is likely to consist of all or some of the following:

1. Doubts, fears and catastrophising the phenomenon of letting one bad thought colour the rest of our thinking.
2. Fantasizing: Imagining the worst is likely to happen and directing all our thoughts to planning for it.
3. Self-deprecating: Letting mistakes and failures lead us to believe we are not good enough.
4. Remembering the Worst: Worrying about something we did in the past that we cannot change.
5. Confusion: Having no clear goals or plans.
6. Reactive Thinking: Thinking is habitual or limiting ways.
7. Distraction: The inability to concentrate and direct our thoughts at will.

Distorted thinking

There are many common types of distorted thinking. Here are four. First, there is lazy thinking where we think in habitual ways rather than in questioning our thoughts. Second, there is compulsive and obsessive thinking where the same thoughts reverberate in our heads again and again. Third, we continually think in musts, should, and ought when we use our brains to judge what we do and how we think. Fourth, there is black-and-white thinking, where we swing from believing that things are wholly good one minute and wholly bad the next. All of these are negative and limiting types of thinking.

Catastrophising

In an untrained person, doubts and fears can form a large part of what passes for thinking. Doubts and fears start small but can feed on themselves until they take over. It is what happens when having left home, the thought occurs that we left the gas or electric on: very soon all our thinking is swamped by this one fear of catastrophe. Here is an anecdote that shows what can happen in the untrained thinking mind.

A woman is driving along the motorway at night. Her thoughts start to race:

"What if I get a puncture on the motorway? I will have to stop and walk though the dark to the nearest garage. Then I will have to ask someone to come out and fix the tyre. They are bound to charge the earth at this time of night. They are bound to look down their nose at me as well. What a nerve?" Just then she arrives at the garage, still thinking these thoughts, fills up her tank, and as she goes to pay her bill, blurts out to the astonished, cashier: "...and you can keep your bloody jack as well."

Conclusion

A good exercise to find out what you habitually think about is to take time out to sit and relax and got down the kind of thoughts you automatically get. A series of such "soil sampling" usually produces a mixture of thoughts: we have thoughts about things on our mind thought about pressing needs such as "I am hungry" and thoughts coming in because of external interference. For many people the content of what normally goes on in their heads jumbled and confused.

"Life does not consist mainly—or even largely—of facts and happenings, it consists mainly of the storm of thoughts—that is forever blowing through one's head." (Mark Twain)

Distraction

The human brain connects to 24,000 ear fibbers, 500,000 touch detectors, and 200,000 temperature sensors 4 million pain sensors. It is no wonder that with this capacity to absorb information, we find hard to concentrate on just one thing at a time. So, instead of focusing, we let our minds wander. Instead of thinking what we need to say, we say the first thing that comes into our heads. Instead of getting to the point, we let our minds go walk about.

Yo-Yo thinking

As well as being distracted, many of us have a tendency to swing from a positive mood to a negative one in what we might call "Yo-Yo thinking": one minute up, the next minute down.

The story is told of the farmer whose ox died and, in panic, went to the wise man of the village and wailed: "I will be ruined. Is not this the worst thing that has ever happened to me." The wise man replied: "May be, maybe not." A few days later, the farmer caught a stray horse on his land and used is to plough the fields in half the time he would have taken with the ox. He returned to the wise man and said: "Is not this the best thing that has ever happened to me?" Again, the wise man replied: "May be so, may be not". There days later, while still overjoyed with his good fortune, the horse threw the farmer's son into a ditch and broke his leg.

Moral: Things are rarely as good-or as bad—as we think.

The self-image

The self-image is the key player in our thoughts. To understand its importance we need to turn. Rene Descartes maxim, "I think therefore and am," and back-to-front into: I AM WHAT I THINK.

Whatever we think we are, we are our self-talk creates our self image. This is because our thoughts are always directed to providing what we want to believe. So, if we think we are stupid at maths, our thoughts will automatically seek evidence that proves it and ignores it and ignore evidence to the contrary. Similarly, if we think we are quite clever at maths, we will seek evidence to prove it. So, the key to releasing the potential of our thinking is to build a confident self-image in which our thinking is a partner in describing who we see ourselves to be.

"Life consists of what a man is thinking about all day." (Ralph Waldo Emerson).

Positive Re-Framing

The reason why a positive self-image and positive thinking succeeds is not only mental. It is also physical. Studies have demonstrated that the neurons in the hippocampus (a part of the brain responsible for day-to-day memory and new learning) can shrink when we are stressed. Dendrites, the connecting wires between brain cells, have been known to permanently shrivel in response to negative thinking. On the other hand, love, affection and happy moods can strengthen these dendrites and enhance our ability to solve intellectual and practical problems.

The negative thinker's answer to:

"Can you play the piano as well as Barenleiom?" is probably, "No, I never could." The positive thinker's answer is "Not Yet."

Expecting the best

Most of us find it easy to worry, but we invariably worry about the worst that might happen to us. By changing our thought direction, we can replace worrying about the worst into worrying about the best.

Worrying positively has the same characteristics as negative worrying: nagging thought patterns; visualizing ourselves in the situation; playing and replaying every possible angle, hearing what we will say, feeling what we will feel, saying to ourselves what we will say.

Olympic javelin thrower Stave Buckle practiced positive worry when he sprained his ankle four weeks before a major competition. Instead of giving up, he mentally practised his throws from his arm-chair until he had made over a thousand throws when the competition came, Backley made the throws he had mentally made and won.

Your brain wants success

For much of the 20th century, it was thought that the brain was a trial and error mechanism: we tried sometime and if it worked, fine. We tried sometime if it did not work, too bad. End of story. We now know differently. The brain is not a trial and error mechanism but a trial and success mechanism. When set a clear goal, it actually seeks out not error but success Error is not incorrect or faulty programming but simply deviation from the correct course. We set our goals. We try, succeed, succeed, succeed, succeed, succeed, make an error, check, adjust, succeed, succeed. Your brain actually wants you to succeed and it lets you know that you can succeed and it lets you know that you can succeed through training your brain to think is constructive, creative and positive ways.

Key Points

1. Untrained thinking is often confusing, distracted and negative.
2. Trained thinking is usually focused, confident and positive.
3. The human brain believes what we let if believe rather than what it knows to be true.
4. Worrying negatively is the same process as worrying positively so just change your focus.
5. "Yo-Yo thinking" is alternatively thinking things are very good or things are very bad.
6. The key to making the best use of our thoughts is to build a positive and confident self-image.

12. Improve Your Memory

Most of us complain at some time about our poor memories—especially when we forget things that are important, such as birthday's anniversaries and meetings. But it is not memory that lets us down. Our brains remember everything we have ever experienced; we know this from near-death experiences, hypnosis and feelings of déjà vu. What is at fault is our ability to recall. Here are 7 ways we can help our ability to recall facts and experiences of the past.

Synaesthesia

Synaesthesia is the association of memory with our senses. Dr. Frank Staub of Yale University demonstrated that you can easily improve your memory, when you link the things you want to remember with a memorable sight, sound, feeling, rate or smell. In one experiment, he wafted the aroma of sweet chocolate over a group of students who were preparing for an exam. On the day of the exam, he released the same aroma while the students were taking the exam. The result was that these students out-performed everyone else

Landmarks

The reason why synaesthesia works is because what we want to recall is associated with a striking landmark. Landmarks do not have to be limited to the five senses. They can be anything emotional, shocking, funny, unexpected, silly, embarrassing, or outrageous. That is why people can recall precisely what they were doing at the time of shocking news events, such as the assassination of John Kennedy or the Death of Diana, Princess of Wales. It is also why we never forget our first day at school, beautiful romantic holidays, and our first teenage kiss.

Rhymes

The Peg system works because we associate a number with a rhyming word, e.g. 8 and "gate" 2 and "glue". The same principle holds true for much more complex pieces of information. So rhymes help us remember that "In fourteen hundred and eighty two Columbus sailed the ocean blue" (and discovered America); that "I before, except after (for spelling words like "believe" and receipt); and that "30 days hath September, April, June and November ......" (For remembering the days of the months)

Mnemonics

Rhyming words like these are known as in mnemonics, after the Greek goddess of memory. Mnemosyne. Another type of mnemonic is associating letters with names in a certain sequence. So, "My very Educated Mother just served us Nine Pizzas" will instantly help you remember the sequence of the nine planes of the solar system, simply be looking at the first letters of each world. Make the sequence: Mercury, Venus, Earth Mars, Jupiter, Saturn, Uranus, Neptune, and Pluto.

The great thing with mnemonics is that you can make up your own sentences for things you want to remember and you can personalize them to your own situations or make them as witty as you want (remember, silly is memorable).

Remembering people's names

The idea of associating something we want to remember with personal, silly, or funny associations is the key to remembering people's names. Let us say you are introduced to a Mr. Lazenby. All you need to do is picture him lying and a summer's day on a Broad and you will remember his name. Similarly, a Mrs. Pakenham could be imagined packing 'em in' a fish factory as Mr. Forsyth could be pictured as a gardener with four scythes. The reason why these associations work is that you are using both sides of your brain. Your left brain holds the name. Your right brain remembers the silly image. Together they help you recall.

Repetition

One of the important keys to all these memory tricks is repetition. When we first collect a new piece of information, it goes straight into our short-term memories. This can only take 8 seconds. The trouble is, the short-term memory is a holding area for new information and unless we move stuff out, it will quickly, be replaced with newer information. Moving information out means moving it into our long-term memories where it can remain indefinitely. The problem here is, it can take anything up to 6 hours to get something firmly embedded. And that is where repetition, review, and replay, come to the rescue.

Some scientists regard memory as the Rosetta stone of the brain. The key unlocks all the secrets of the mind. In an age of information, where most people are knowledge workers of one sort or another having a good memory and being able to make the most of what you know is not just nice to have; it is essential.

Key Points

1. When we forget something it is not because of a poor memory but because of our inability to recall.
2. There are various ways to increase our power of recall, all making use of our imaginative right brains.
3. Events that are shocking, emotional and silly stay in the memory. Longer than things that are mundane and normal
4. You can remember an event more vividly when you associate it with one or more of your five senses, such as smell or taste.
5. Mnemonics are one of the best ways to remember lengthy or complex information by associating numbers with rhyming sounds.
6. To move information from your short-term memory into your long-term memory, you need to repeat if enough times to make it stick.

13. Blocks to Thinking

Thinking, like communicating, is one of those functions we think we should be good at because we do it all the time, do it without effort and have done it for all of our waking lives. But there is a difference between just doing something like thinking or communicating and doing it well. Just as with communicating effectively, what stops us from thinking effectively for much of the time are the perceptual, emotional, cultural and environmental blocks that get in the way.

Here are 7 of those blocks:

Assumptions

When we assume, we often make an "ass" out of "U" and "me". Assumptions are examples of lezzy thinking. We simply do not wait to get all the information we need to come to the right conclusions. There is the story of the customer at the bank who after cashing a cheque and turning to leave, returns and says: "Excuse me, I think you made a mistake." The cashier responds, "I am sorry but there is nothing I can do. You should have counted it. Once you walk away we are no longer responsible." Whereupon the customer replies: "Well, okay. Thanks for the extra $20."

Tip: When you feel yourself wanting to draw conclusions, just wait until you have all the information.

See things from other points of view

A truly open mind is willing to accept that not do other people have other just as valid points of view from theirs, but that these other points of view may be more valid. A story is told that the modernist painter Pablo Picasso was once travelling on a train across Spain when he got into conversation with rich businessman who was dismissive of modern art. As evidence that modern art did not properly represent reality, he took out a photo of his wife from his wallet and said: "This is how my wife should look not in some silly stylized representation. Picasso took the photo, studied it for a few moments and asked: "This is your wife?" The businessman proudly nodded. "She is very small," observed Picasso Wryly.

Tip: Do not have a monopoly on how things are. Things are not always what they seem. Be ready to consider other points of view.

Thinking and Doing

It is part of Western intellectual tradition that the thinking part of a decision is separate from the implementation part of the decision, as if the decision was one thing and the implementation something quite different. Hence the gulf between those who take decisions, often in positions of authority, and those who carry them out : thinkers and doers. mIn oriental philosophy, which has a much longer tradition than western philosophy, the gap is not understood. Here there is no gulf between thinking and doing. There is only process. A decision and its implementation are part and parcel of the same thing. This means that the decision can be changed as the implementation proceeds, just as the method of implementation can be changed if the decision is reviewed in the light of new information.

Tip: Involve implementers in the decision process.

Get rid of lazy thinking habits

Habit can be a major stumbling block to clear thinking and another example of laziness. Try this experiment. Write down the Scottish Surnames MacDonald, Macpherson and MacDougall and ask someone to pronounce them. Now follow these with the word Machinery and see what happens. Most people are likely to miss-pronounce it. This is because we tend to think in habitual ways and do not like what does not fit.

Think like a child

Research shows that the number of synapses or connections, in the brain is greater in a child of two than in an average adult. The reason for this is that a child of two has no limiting world view, as adults do. It is like a sculptor who starts off a large block of lay that can become anything. As he gradually removes the clay, the possibilities in his sculpture become, less and less until it represents just what he is looking for. If we use our brain like a child, accepting without judgement We can actually half and reverse the brain ageing process and become fully open-minded again.

Tip: With the right stimulus and a passion for wonder, you can think like a child again.

See the detail as well as the big picture

There is a poem by John Godtrey Saxe called "The blind men and the Elephant". It tells how six blind men of Indostan go to see an elephant and each try to work out what it is from touching it. One blind man touches the tusk, another trunk, another tails and so on. Of course, not being able to see the whole elephant, they disagree about what the animal is. When we see the detail and the full picture, it is easier to give everything its right context.

Tip: Try to keep the big picture in front of you while looking at the details. It will help to put everything in its proper place.

Think for yourself

Taking time out to think is still frowned on in many organisations that prize activity over creativity. People who work in creativity—constrained organizations are likely to think the way they are supposed to think, or as others think or as has always been the way to think. It is like the blinkered thinking that Hans Christian Anderson describes in his story of "The Emperor's new clothes". Everyone in the land refuses to see that the emperor is naked and has been duped into believing he is wearing a splendid constume for his coronation. Only a young boy who has been ill and not party to the cultural brain washing can see the truth and cries out. "Look, everyone, the Emperor is wearing no clothes."

Tip: Do not let others tell you how to think. When others ask your opinion, tell it to them straight.

Time to Think

One of the biggest stumbling-blocks to thinking is that, in many organizations, we still do not recognize that it is sometimes more important than activity. Here is a story that illustrates an anti-thinking attitude the car-maker Henry Ford hired an efficiency expert to go through his plant. He said: "Find the unproductive people. Tell me who they are and I will fire them". The expert made his rounds with his clipboard in hand and finally returned to Henry Ford's office with his report. "I have found a problem with one of your managers," he said "Every time I walked past his office; he was sitting with his fact propped on the desk doing nothing.

I definitely think you should consider getting rid of him. "When Ford asked who the man was, he shook his head and said: "I cannot fire him. I pay that man to do nothing but think. And that is what he is doing."

Each of us has the power to think clearly. It is part of our natural make-up as human beings. The trouble is that, too often, we block our natural thinking ability and so make errors in judgement. By unblocking your thinking by not judging, not making assumptions, and not blindly accepting the views of others, you can access the full creativity of your thinking.

Key Points

1. We often make wrong assumptions about what we see because of prejudice and false expectations.
2. We each see the world differently because of our thoughts; every "thing is a think".
3. Thinking like a child is more open and creative because it is not layered with years of learning and habit.
4. Culturally-accepted ways of thinking can sometimes limit us to thinking in familiar ways.
5. Well-directed and well-trained thinking is always more productive than activity.
6. Successful enterprises need original thinking if they are to avoid blindly following the thinking of the majority.

14. Logical Thinking

Logical thinking is to think on the basis of knowledge, what we know, and certainties, what we can prove. The past two centuries have witnessed an unparatted reliance on the logical approach to thinking. It is the basis on which modern technology is founded. But the flew in logical thinking is that it relies on the conscious brain and this is the most limited and vulnerable part of our thinking.

Left-brain thinking

Logical thinking is the part of the brain that relates to its-left-hand side for "left" and "L" "Logical". It was Professor Roger Sperry of the University of California who discovered that different sides of the brain were responsible for different functions. He discovered that the left-brain:

- governs the right side of the body,
- governs the right field of vision,
- deals with input sequentially,

- perceives the parts more than the whole,
- perceives time,
- is the seat of verbal skills,
- is the seat of logical and analytical thinking
- Sets goals, plans and reviews: the managerial mind.
- Formulates evocative language.

The left side of the brain is the chattering mind, thriving on, but limited by information.

Right brain thinking

Just as he explained the working of the logical, left sided brain, so Roger Sperry also discovered that the right-hand side is responsible for romantic types of thinking. In contrast to the left, the discovered that the right brain.

- Governs the left side of the body.
- Governs the left field of vision.
- Deals with inputs simultaneously.
- Perceives the whole more than the parts.
- Perceives space.
- Is the seat of visual skills?
- Is the seat of intuitive and kinaesthetic perception?
- Is responsible for imaginations and visualization.

Managerial thinking

Managerial thinking tends to use the functions of the left brain more than those of the right brain. The sort of workplace issues that use left-brain thinking are analysing and detecting faults in mechanical processes through collecting, checking and testing information; investigation problems of the "What went wrong ?" variety; learning from how things have been done in the past to improve the way we do them next time and obtaining information that answers "what?" "Where?" "Who?" and "why" questions all of these issues relay information and on information being correct, complete and understood.

Logical thinking

Logical (or left brain) thinking comes into its own when we are working with verifiable and reasonably certain information.

This is information we can be sure about because it has been confirmed scientifically. Using "Scientific" information allows us to develop our knowledge by making logical deductions. It is the kind of thinking used in playing games of chess, (where there are quite definite rules) and solving puzzles for which there is an answer.

Logical thinking uses 5 steps:

1. A clear goal or solution;
2. Systematic planning;
3. Using information;
4. Reasoning;
5. Checking conclusions.

Smart goals

The first step in logical thinking is a clear goal. Working towards clear goals is often described by the mnemonic SMART.

These are goals which are Specific, Measurable, Achievable, Realistic and Time-bounded. For example, it may be a department's goal to produce 30 tons of products a day from 29 tons after upgrading its machinery. SMART goals are managerial goals. They lend themselves to plans and the application of a step-by-step thought-and-action process. Clear goals work from a known starting point (that is, now) in a series of steps and sequences until the goal is reached. SMART goals assume that the future will be the same as now, that resources will be the same as now, that resources will star the same and that nothing will interrupt the execution of the plan. If anything changes, then so will the SMART goals.

Systematic Planning

Systematic planning is the second step in the SMART process towards a goal. We know the "What?" because we have defined a clear goal. Systematic planning tells us the "how?" to get us there. Systematic planning aims to find the correct method, the correct procedure, the correct system that can logically take us to our goal. In SMART goal thinking, planning is "Systematic" because we can try it out in different circumstances, repeated by and with different kinds of information. If is like a computer programme into which we type our formula and apply our information to come up with THE answer.

Using Information

The remaining steps are the SMART process involves using our left-sided brains to work towards our goals. Information is key to this process. We need to group it, organize it, rank it, fit it into the bigger picture, and make connections with it. It needs to be as accurate and verifiable as possible or else there can be no basis for further logical thought. Where information is uncertain, difficult to check, subject to change, not easy to understand, then it is of limited use.

The limits of information

Logical thinking relies wholly an how reliable your information is. But is a fast-changing world, information presents as with a number of problems.

There is too much of it

We are bombarded today with huge amounts of information, much of it contradictory. It is calculated that one copy of the British Sunday Times Contains in it more information than medieval man would have had access to in a life time.

It gets distorted easily

All knowledge comes to us via someone else's perception and is fettered by our own perception. Even the most unbiased of television news.-readers cannot avoid an occasional voice inflexion or raised eyebrow when they deliver a story. We can never be absolutely sure of the motives and thinking behind the information we receive. "Never ask a hairdresser if you need a haircut."

It is in complete

We can never know whether the information 'we receive' is complete or incomplete. In the hours after the death of Diana, Princess of Wales, in a car accident in 1997 everyone believed that she had been a victim of pursuing photographers.

Later it was discovered that her chauffeur had excessive levels of alcohol in his blood.

It is quickly outdated

In today's world of instant access to information via World-wide communications knowledge quickly becomes outdated, obsolete and forgotten. All through history, when a craftsman learned his trade after a period of four, five or six years of apprenticeship, he had learned everything he would ever need to know. It would be sufficient for the rest of his working life. Today, this is no longer enough. We need updates every few years to keep abreast of what is happening in our chosen field. The giant American Corporation, General Electric, has specialized that a newly-recounted engineer's knowledge will be out of date within five years of starting in the job.

Our conscious brains can only hold a limited amount of information

Our knowledge-holding brains—the conscious thinking parts—is only capable of holding a limited amount of data at any one time. Most of us find it hard to keep more than about 7 or 8 cards from a pack of playing cards, allow them 15 seconds to memorize them in their heads; and then ask them to turn the cards over and recall them. Very few people can successfully remember every single card.

Now contrast this with the sub-conscious brain which stores every single experience and thought that we have ever had and still has room for a huge amount more.

The logical or scientific, approach to thinking relies on information about the world around us. From it, we can create the most wonderful inventions and manifestations. But, in a fast-paced world, this information is quickly out-of-date, quickly in accurate, and quickly useless. If we are to rely on logical thinking to succeed in life, then we need to be masters of left-brain thinking.

Key Points

1. Ordered thinking is thinking that is analytical, sensible and systematic.
2. The left side of the brain is the seat of logical thinking.
3. The right side of the brain is the seat of imaginative thinking.
4. Logical thinking allows us to make incremented progress based on verifiable information.
5. While logical thinking relies on facts and information, information itself can be unreliable and undecorated.

The analytical conscious brain is limited in the amount of information it can hold while the creative subconscious is unlimited.

15. Creative Thinking

In our Western systems of thinking, there is a strong bias towards using the left-brain. We tend to prefer ideas that fit preconceived patterns, systems that have been proved and solutions that are low-risk. But in a time of change, where we need to solve major intractable problems, we need to be more creative and instead of known thinking and known solutions, develop new thinking and new solutions, i.e. using the right brain. Here are of ways to be more creative.

Think like a Child

As adults we tend to think in a conditioned way aimed at showing how clever we are. Yet, as Children, we are simply spontaneous and for more curious in our thinking. To recapture your childhood curiosity, allow yourself to just wonder at things, to be completely present in the here and now, and to detach yourself from what you thought was real.

- Why are leaves green? Who is Father Christmas? What makes us yawn?
- Where do people come from? Why do we have to go to sleep? What is at the end of a rainbow?
- What happens when we die? What makes us laugh?
- Why do people fight?
- What makes the light go on?
- Where do animals go when they die? Why do we have to work?

Be more curious

The search for new answers to old problems starts with being curious about the problem and looking at it with fresh eyes. Sigmund Freud said that such curiosity came more naturally to children than adults. Other great inventors have also recognized the importance to creative thinking of being curious about the world. This is how Leonardo da Vinci described his endless curiosity "I roamed the country side searching for answers to things I did not understand. Why shells existed on the tops of mountains along with the imprint of coral and plant and sea weed found in the sea. Why the thunder lasts a longer time than that which causes it and why immediately on its creation the lightening becomes visible to the eye while circles of water from around the spot which has been struck by a storm and why a bird sustains itself in the air. These questions and other strange phenomenon engaged my thought throughout my life.

Play with ideas

The route to creativity is to see things in ways that nobody has seen before. Albert Einstein, the father of modern science imagined how his theory of relativity could work by lying on a grassy hillside and picturing himself riding on a sunbeam into the universe. Steven Spielberg, director of the science ficition film "Close Encounters of a Third kind" imagined the spaceship he used in the film by standing upside down on his car bonnet and looking at the night lights of Los Angles.

The great comedian, Buster Keaton, Was one of the most original and inspired creative thinkers of the era of silent movies. He was once asked onto the set of a film to help a director who had put a character into a predicament from which there appeared no logical escape. The character had to get out of a room through one of two doors. One door led into an adjoining room where there was a group of people whom he did not want to meet. The other door led to the outside where the plot had inconsiderably placed a vicious barking dog.

Without even stopping to think, Keaton provided a solution. All the character had to do was to take the door off its hinges, open it a bit to let the dog into the room and then escape the snatches of the dog's teeth by swivelling the door around full circle, leaving the dog on the inside and himself on the outside.

Make new connections

To be innovative does not require a university degree; it simply requires making a connection between existing ideas. For instance, did you know that ice-cream was invented in 2000 BC yet it took another 3900 years for someone to come up with the idea of a cone? It is when you take two seemingly undated items and use the spark of creativity that inventiveness happens. This is what one inventor did when he was puzzling one lazy morning in bed about how to invest the perfect egg-cup that would adjust to fit all shapes and sizes of egg. Suddenly a bed-spring collapsed with a twanging sound, and the perfect egg-cup, a coiled metal spring to support any kind of egg, was invented.

Try this trick for yourself. Put together two unconnected objects in the room right now such as a stapler and a pair of scissors and find a use for them.

Be a little illogical

One of the least logical thinking systems in philosophy is the oriental school of Zen Buddhism. Zen attempts to go beyond the confines of logic to enlightenment.

Zen means "meditation," It takes problems and presents those in ways that make you think. One "Koan," or problem, with no intellectual solution, asks: "What is the sound of one hand clapping?" and another: "When a finger points at the moon, the imbecile looks at the finger."

A Zen tale tells of a Zen master who comes across a disciple walking on water. "What are you doing?" he cried. "Crossing the river," replied the disciple. "Come with me," ordered the master and together they walked a great distance until they found a ferryman. As they climbed on to the boat, the master said pointedly: "This is the way to cross a river."

Laugh more

Tom Peters says that the creativity of a workplace can be measured by a laugh meter, i.e. how much people in the organization laugh. Humour is one of the greatest creative devices. It golts us out of our normal patterns and puts ideas together that should not go together. It has been found that after listening to comedy tapes, students' ability to solve problems rises by 60% "I like non-sense; it wakes up the brain cells. Pantosy is a necessary ingredient in living. It is a way of looking at life through the wrong end of a telescope and that enables you to laugh at life's realities."

Think outside your limits

Many of the products we take for granted today are the result of people thinking outside their limits. John Lynn recalls attending a computer conference in the 1980's at a hotel when someone joked that the next thing they would be thinking of would be computerised doors. When he went back to the same hotel 20 years later all the doors used computer-programmed key cards. You can practice this kind of thinking with these pointers:

- Let go of old ways of seeing, thinking and doing.
- Question what you see, remembering that we distort what we see with our perceptions.
- Have a clear understanding of what outcome you desire but divorce the outcome from the method.
- Be aware that thinking in familiar patterns can limit your options of what is possible.
- Free yourself from grudging your own ideas.
- Find a stream of creative ideas by thinking more like a child.

- Take risks and dare to do things differently.
- Be absolutely sure that you will succeed. When we think vertically, we limit ourselves to what we already know, what has been done before and the old ways of thinking.

We can build upwards as a result but our progress is more of the same or vertical evolution. The alternative to vertical thinking is lateral, or horizontal, thinking. It is also outrageous thinking curious thinking the unthinkable and creative thinking.

Key Points

1. Creative thinking at all levels has become a necessary for organizations to stay ahead in the modern business world.
2. When you are in the wrong hole, it is no good digging deeper; you need to get another hole.
3. Children tend to be more curious about their world than adults.
4. One simple way to increase your creativity is to make new connections between unrelated objects and ideas.
5. Creativity requires as to open up our minds to experiences and ideas we do not usually have.
6. A creative work place is invariably one in which there is a large amount of honour and irreverence

16. Brainstorming

Brainstorming is the most widely known and used method of group thinking with others has a number of advantages Over thinking alone. It increases the number of ideas we can have; it increases the quality of ideas; it allows us to scrutinize ideas more carefully; and it ensures that ideas that get supported have a better chance of successful implementation.

Brainstorming—Start

The name "brainstorming" was originally used in the 1950's by Alex Osborn, the founder of an advertising firm. The aim of brain storming is to produce the largest quantity of ideas concerning a problem in the shortest possible time. Osborn proposed 5 rules in brainstorming:

1. No evaluation of ideas.
2. Wild ideas to be encouraged.
3. Quantity of ideas is important.

4. Participants should build on each Other's ideas.
5. Apart from the above four, there are no other rules.

A Brainstorming Session

A brain storming session can be applied to both problems which have a single solution waiting to be discovered, e.g. a machine fault, as well as situations where there in no known solution, e.g. how to improve your customer relations. The following are the steps in a brainstorming session:

(a) Select a scribe to write down the ideas (speedily).
(b) Create a relaxed climate.
(c) Start with a brainteaser to warm people up
(d) Use flip charts to record ideas that everyone can see.
(e) Ensure nobody dominates.
(f) Encourage a free flow of ideas.
(g) Use a facilitator to guide and support.
(h) Have a set time limit, say of 10-15 minutes.
(i) Only evaluate ideas once you have finished.

Sparking

The first stage in brain storming is to spark as many different ideas as you can about the problem. In response to the problem, "How can we improve the paperwork systems in the office?" These ideas might be suggested:

- buy a concertina file;
- Colour-code the paper files;
- microfilm them;
- burn them;
- Place them on computer;
- Code them according to the Cyrillic alphabet;
- hang them on a line;
- put them in pigeon holes;
- sent them back to where they come from;
- Put them in colour coded waste bins.

Paradoxical Intention

Paradoxical intention is a brain storming technique for sparking more ideas by deliberately thinking of ways to make the problem worse. In the example of how to improve the paperwork in an office, you could add the following to the list.

- tell everyone to put things in writing;
- mix the files up;
- leave them in untidy piles;
- remove the filing cabinets;
- do not have a clerk;
- Collect others' bills as well and soon.

It is possible that one idea might paradoxically have the basis of a solution: in this case, the office could agree to collect others bills and twin itself into an archive-center.

Seeding

Seeding is a brain storming technique that takes a word that has nothing to do with the problem and seeing what connections you can make between it and the problem. For example, if we were looking, at ideas to improve the way we organize office systems, we could at random propose the word "breakfast". This could then seed the following ideas:

- keep all the paperwork files in empty cornflakes packets;
- sort the papers out over breakfast;
- stick the papers together with marmalade;
- hold a breakfast meeting to discuss ideas;
- devise a filing cabinet in the shape of a breakfast bar;
- have a daily breakfast-time clear out of files;
- Have a deadline on all incoming paperwork by breakfast time each day and so on.

Wording

Wording is a brainstorming technique that takes each word or group of words that spellout what the problem exactly is and seeing what ideas each word sparks. In the case of ideas to improve the way we organize our office paperwork systems, following might be suggested:

"How...": are there different methods we could try out? How do others do it? How are we in this mess?

"Can...": are we capable? Do we need expert help? What skills do not we have that we need?

"We...": is there someone else we can pass the problem to? Do we need to change?

"Organize...": Why do we need to organize the papers? "The paperwork...": why papers? Can't we computerize?

"In the office...": Why do they have to stay in the office? Why do they have to come to this office?

An Example of Brainstorming: The Honey Pot

Pacific, Power and Light (PP and L) is the electric utility responsible for providing power to the Northwest cascade mountain area of the United States. This area faces severe weather in spring and autumn each year resulting in heavy ice deposits on power transmission lines. Lines frequently comedown under the weight of the ice the Company's method of removing the iced lines is to send linesmen through the snow and up the icy pylons and to physically shake the ice off the lines. It is a long, arduous, costly and unpleasant way of dealing with the problem.

A brainstorming session is hold to look at what can be done. The PP and L group spend a whole morning looking at the problem but get nowhere. Frustrated and running out of ideas, the group decide to take a coffee break. During coffee, Bill, a linesman, has everyone in fits of laughter.

"Last week I was chased by a bear. It even climbed a pylon after me."

As the laughter dies down, someone suggests. "Why don't we get the bears to climb for us? "How it is?"

"We could put honey pots on top of the pylons".

"No, the raccoons would get there first."

"Anyway we would need helicopters to put the pots in place and they would frighten the bears" says one of the secretaries. "I remember the vibrations from helicopters in the Vietnam war when I was a nurse.

There was silence as everyone realises they have struck gold.

Today it is standard practice in PP and L to use helicopters to remove ice from frozen cable lines.

Brain Wonting

Brainstorming is not always the best way to produce neither lots of ideas nor lots of good ideas. That is because group dynamics often affect how people contribute. A group with low trust is never going to do well using the standard approach to brain storming. The way round this is to use the related technique of Brain Writing. In Brain writing, the group does not work as a group; they work individually by writing their ideas down on a sheet of paper and then take turns in passing these rounds to others to add to the list. This way, people can share ideas among musty and quickly and still come up with a large quantity of solutions to choose from.

Brainstorming, and brain writing, is recognized as two of the least ways to use groups to improve thinking and creativity.

That is because everyone has the potential to be creative and imaginative rather than just the so-called "clever". Not only do you get more ideas and more options, you also get involvement and commitment to the final decisions.

Key Points

1. You are likely to get more ideas from working with a group than from working on your own.
2. The drawback to working with group is that others may have different agendas from you.
3. For group work to succeed there must first be agreement on how the group is to work and make decisions.
4. Brain-storming sessions should be held in a relaxed and non-judgemental climate.
5. Be willing to try out crazy ideas in a brainstorming session.
6. Brain writing is an improvement on brain storming when a group is not cohesive.

17. Decision—Making

Managers, team leaders and their staff can take as many as a hundred or more decisions in the course of a day, each day and every day. Many of these decisions are, of course, no more than automatic responses to familiar situations in which they have to choose between two or three options. However, from time to time, we all have to take decisions on which the course of our future and that of others depends. Then, it is a question of making sure they are right. Here are 7 principles to guide you in right decision- making.

Time them

There are two taps which people fall into when making decisions: making them too soon and making them too late. Some people make decisions to swiftly and without due thought. This may be because they are uncomfortable with the tension that is created when a decision has to be made but they do not have all the information needed. Instead of living with tension they make the decision before time. Other people delay making decisions because they fear making a mistake or feat the changes that will result. The best decisions are hot iron decisions: those that are well-timed, which you make when the iron is hot and the time is right.

Knowing where to strike

Decisions should be made with the precision that comes from knowledge and knowing where and when to strike. A famous shipyard in the 1970's, one day before the maiden voyage of their biggest ship to date. She would not start. There is something wrong with the boiler. Checked every nut, tightened every bolt. Still nothing happen. They sent for an expert. A guy from Hamburg scratched his beard. He Said: "My fees Rs. 1000."

The foreman nodded frantically. "Stand back," said the expert. He gave the boiler an almighty wallop with his hammer. It hiccupped, barped, chugged into life. The foreman stood again aghast. You will charge Rs. 1000 for one thump with a hammer?" "No" said the expert. "For one thump with the hammer charged one pound and for knowing where to thump, nine hundred and ninety nine."

Align them

The more decisions you make consciously the more you can align them with your goals and purposes. Studies show that the average person makes 612 decisions a day. Each one takes us closer or further from our ultimate goals in life. In a weak that means 4,900 decisions. In a year, 2, 54,800. Results are cumulative. Strategic thinking means looking at how your decisions today affect your tomorrows. When your decisions are in alignment with what is important to you, then life becomes meaningful, productive and satisfying.

Balance them

There are three balancing acts to be aware of in taking a good decision. They are : Too care and not care. Do all your worrying before the decision and once a decision has been taken, stop worrying.

- Think and act. Too much thinking puts off the action; too much action may be at the expense of thought. Seek the right balance.

- Look before you leap and leap before you look. See the possible risks of your decision but, once decided, take the plunge with courage.

Act when you have to

You should only make decisions when you have to.

- Don't make a decision unless you have two or more equally valid options.
- Don't make a decision if it's somebody else's responsibility.
- Don't make a decision unless there is disagreement.
- Don't make a decision about irrelevant matters.
- Don't make a decision if it cannot be turned into action. "If there's one thing I have learned in politics, it is: never make a decision until you have to." (Margaret Thatcher)

Use a decision-making model

There are no guaranteed ways to make a perfect decision. As Ian Wilson said, "No amount of sophistication is going to alley the fact that all your knowledge is about the past and all your decisions are about the future." However, there are decision making systems that can help us in making important decisions. Here is a selection of the best models.

Decision Trees

Decision trees are diagrams which consider the different options of a decision by weighing up the likely outcomes and considering how desirable and probable they are.

Let us say you wanted to start up in business but could not decide whether to start now or in a year's time. On the tree you would first state what the outcomes could be of each course. For "starting up now," the outcomes could be "getting into the market early" which would be highly desirable and highly probable; and "Over-stretching" which would be quite probable and not at all desirable. On the other hand, for leaving it for a year," the outcomes could be "missing the market," which would be very desirable and quite probable; and "better preparation" which would be fairly desirable but only fairly probable. Weighing the options up, it is clear what the best course is.

Pros and Cons

One of the simplest ways to make a decision is to take a piece of paper and draw a line down the middle of the page. On the right side, list the pluses. On the left side, list the minuses. Weigh up the respective merits of each side, perhaps by giving each factor a weighting, and then decide. Aligned to this method are cost- benefit analyses, and force-field analyses.

Toss a Coin

When all other factors are equal and we cannot make up our minds whether to say "Yes" or "No", "This way or that way," the simplest solution may be to toss a coin. It is worth noting that when Albert Einstein had to make a choice, he would toss a coin and as soon as it landed, he would ask himself how he felt. If good, he would go with it; if bad, he would go against it.

The Equivalent Urn and the Probability Wheel

The equivalent urn and the probability wheel combine the ratings of the pros and cons method of decision-taking with pure chance. In the equivalent urn, which is any large container that can hold ping-pong balls, place black balls for every disadvantage in an option and white balls for every advantage in an option? You can rate each factor from 1 to 10 on the scale of desirability of probability and mark the rating on the balls. Now shuffle the balls and pick one out of the urn (or the best of three). Use these to decide whether to go for it or not. The probability wheel is similar to the equivalent urn, except that the options are drawn on the spokes of a spinning. Wheel and Weighted according to their rating.

The wheel is spun and the spoke that points to the winning arrow is the option to take.

Parent, Adult, Child

The Parent Adult-Child decision-making model uses the Parent, Adult, Child concepts from Transactional Analysis to illustrate three approaches to making a decision.

Let us say we have seen a book that we want to buy at £ 29.00.

- The child in us wants it; we love the thought of owning it, feeling it, enjoying it, the thought of owning it thrill us.
- The internal Parent in us asks us what we should do, wondering whether the money could not be better spent elsewhere and whether it is not a bit of a waste of money.

- The Adult in us weighs up dispassionately what the pros and cons are in the light of our other needs and goals.

We can now make an informed decision whether to buy it or not.

Six thinking Hats

Edward de Bono's "Six thinking Hats" and "Six thinking Shoes" models are attempts to break out of traditional, logical decision-making. Both models use clothing and their colours to prompt us to think in certain ways when making a decision.

- White hat: White is neutral and objective and like white paper, conveys simple facts.
- Black hat Black is judgmental like the black hat a judge put on when passing the death sentence.
- Red hat: Red is fire, warmth and energy and represents intuitive thought. It is the colour of a witch is hat.
- Yellow hat: Yellow is the colour of a straw boaster and is summery, positive and optimistic.
- Green hat: Green, the colour of a gardener's hat, represents new life and new ideas.

Top Tips for Your Tech Interview

You've landed the interview — great job! Whether you are diving into the job hunt for the first time or returning to the drawing board after years as a developer, tech interviews can still seem incredibly daunting. You have put in all of the hard work, but the uncertainty of the process can make even seasoned professionals nervous. But with the right preparation and approach, you can spend less time worrying and more time impressing. Check out the following tips to help your skills shine.

Do Your Research

A little bit of research can go a long way when it comes to prepping for your interview? Look up the company on Glassdoor, and if you know the name of your interviewer, research them on LinkedInahead of time. Knowing whether your interviewer is an HR manager, a project lead, or a senior developer will help you set better expectations for what kinds of questions will be asked. Researching the types of questions that may come up can go a long way as well. Check out Geek Interview to explore a database of interview questions categorized by specific roles.

Practice Makes Perfect

Live coding and technical testing are often key components of the technical interview process. Practicing timed and uncertain questions can help you nail this segment on interview day. Check out Leet Code to explore a bank of practice coding interview questions and Hacker Rank to complete a range of timed challenges. Consider getting up in front of a whiteboard and having a friend ask you some questions, as you may be asked to do some live coding during the interview. Practicing all scenarios will help you get comfortable with whatever might be thrown your way.

Polish Your Portfolio

Having a great portfolio of projects that demonstrate your skills will go a long way in convincing an employer that you know your stuff. Projects should demonstrate marketable skills and highlight your abilities in the languages required in the position you are interviewing for. Additionally, projects should demonstrate complexity, including 3-5 distinct features. These can include things like integrating with an API, interacting with a database, or having a login or authentication component. Consider using a framework such as Angular or React for front end sites and projects. The number of projects you have is not nearly as important as the complexity and professionalism of any given project. Having your portfolio organised and easily accessible will help make a great impression with your interviewer.

During The Interview

Take a Pause

When the interviewer asks a question, whether technical or not, take a moment to think and consider your answer before beginning a response. Particularly for tricky technical problems, taking a pause shows depth of thought. If you feel the need to answer immediately, throw out a filler phrase like "That's a great question" or repeating the question to give yourself time to think.

Break It Down

When it comes to technical questions, employers often are as interested in your thought process as they are in your final answer. Don't assume any knowledge (unless your interviewer says to) and articulate every step of your thought process. This will help make your answer clear and keep you on track.

Confidence Is Key

Even if you are uncertain in an answer, put your best foot forward when solving a problem. Avoid self-deprecating humor...giving yourself the benefit of the doubt will make your interviewer more likely to do that same.

Ask Questions

This advice applies both during and after the interview. If you are unsure about a question, ask clarifying questions to ensure you are zoning in on the right things. Additionally, ask questions of your interviewer after the interview to highlight your depth of knowledge and interest in the company and the opportunity. For technical roles, showing an interest and knowledge in technical team dynamics will help contribute to your credibility. Consider asking questions about scrum, agile, team dynamics, and current/future projects to demonstrate your willingness to be a team player.

After The Interview

Follow Up

Be sure to send a thank-you note to your interviewers after the interview. Generally, you can send this note via email, but make sure to tailor it specifically to topics from the interview, including ideas you may have for improving the company's site, or further examples of work you highlighted in the interview.

Bonus Tip

No matter the outcome, every interview is a learning opportunity. If you find certain questions tripping you up, take note, look-up answers after the interview, and keep practicing similar problems to be better prepared for you next opportunity!

❑❑❑